*Board of Governors*
*of the John Carter Brown Library*

T. KIMBALL BROOKER

J. CARTER BROWN

VINCENT J. BUONANNO

NANCY CARNEY

GEORGE D. EDWARDS, JR.

VARTAN GREGORIAN, *Chairman*

DWIGHT HEATH

ARTEMIS A. W. JOUKOWSKY

FREDERICK LIPPITT

JOSÉ E. MINDLIN

CLINTON I. SMULLYAN, JR.

FRANK S. STREETER

MERRILY TAYLOR

CHARLES C. TILLINGHAST, JR.

LADISLAUS VON HOFFMANN

WILLIAM B. WARREN

CHARLES H. WATTS, II

SPANISH HISTORICAL
WRITING ABOUT THE NEW WORLD
1493–1700

*The publication of this work was
assisted by grants from the following agencies:*

COMITÉ CONJUNTO HISPANO-NORTEAMERICANO PARA
LA COOPERACIÓN CULTURAL Y EDUCATIVA

FUNDACIÓN RAMÓN ARECES

PROGRAM FOR CULTURAL COOPERATION BETWEEN
SPAIN'S MINISTRY OF CULTURE AND
UNITED STATES' UNIVERSITIES

THE CONSULATE GENERAL OF SPAIN
(BOSTON, MASSACHUSETTS)

AMTRACO L.P.


*The publication of
this work has been endorsed by:*

CHRISTOPHER COLUMBUS
QUINCENTENARY JUBILEE COMMISSION

SPAIN '92 FOUNDATION

# SPANISH HISTORICAL WRITING ABOUT THE NEW WORLD

## 1493–1700

By ANGEL DELGADO-GOMEZ

UNIVERSITY OF NOTRE DAME

*with a Bibliographical Supplement by*

SUSAN L. NEWBURY

*Including a List of Editions & Translations*
*Published before* 1801

PROVIDENCE, RHODE ISLAND
*Published by* THE JOHN CARTER BROWN LIBRARY
*in Recognition of the Quincentenary Year*
1992

COPYRIGHT © 1994 BY THE JOHN CARTER BROWN LIBRARY

ALL RIGHTS RESERVED

THIS WORK MAY NOT BE REPRODUCED
IN PART OR WHOLE, IN ANY FORM OR MEDIUM, FOR
ANY PURPOSE, WITHOUT PRIOR PERMISSION IN WRITING
FROM THE COPYRIGHT OWNER.
CORRESPONDENCE SHOULD BE DIRECTED TO THE
JOHN CARTER BROWN LIBRARY, BOX 1894,
PROVIDENCE, RHODE ISLAND 02912

ISBN 0-916617-40-8

THE JOHN CARTER BROWN LIBRARY IS AN
INDEPENDENTLY FUNDED AND ADMINISTERED CENTER FOR
ADVANCED RESEARCH IN HISTORY AND THE
HUMANITIES AT BROWN UNIVERSITY

# CONTENTS

| | |
|---|---|
| LIST OF ILLUSTRATIONS | *page* ix |
| PREFACE  *by Norman Fiering* | xi |
| ACKNOWLEDGMENTS | xiv |
| INTRODUCTION  *by Angel Delgado-Gomez* | 3 |
| I  *Novus Orbis: The Early Accounts* | 7 |
| II  *Into the Mainland: The Conquest of Mexico* | 14 |
| III  *About and by the Indians: Ethnography of Mexico* | 23 |
| IV  *The Land of the Inca: The Conquest of Peru* | 32 |
| V  *The Continental Empire* | 42 |
| VI  *The Overall View: The Quest for a General History* | 52 |
| VII  *Church History* | 62 |
| VIII  *Biography* | 71 |
| IX  *Literature* | 77 |
| EPILOGUE:  *The New World and the World* | 86 |
| RELATED SECONDARY SOURCES | 89 |
| BIBLIOGRAPHICAL SUPPLEMENT  *by Susan L. Newbury* | 91 |
|    PREFACE | 93 |
|    REFERENCES | 95 |
|    KEY TO LOCATION SYMBOLS | 97 |
|    BIBLIOGRAPHICAL DESCRIPTIONS OF THE WORKS FEATURED IN THE EXHIBITION | 99 |
|    PRE-1801 EDITIONS AND TRANSLATIONS | 119 |

## LIST OF ILLUSTRATIONS

FRONTISPIECE: Map of America, PEDRO DE CIEZA DE LEÓN, *La prima parte dell'istorie del Peru.*   page 2

1. First depiction of Columbus's "discovery," *Epistola* (Basel).   9
2. Title page, ENCISO, *Suma de geographia.*   11
3. Solar tables, ENCISO, *Suma de geographia.*   13
4. Illustration of means of fire-making, FERNÁNDEZ DE OVIEDO Y VALDÉS, *De la natural hystoria de las Indias.*   14
5. Illustration of hammock, FERNÁNDEZ DE OVIEDO Y VALDÉS, *De la natural hystoria de las Indias.*   14
6. Plan of Tenochtitlan, CORTÉS, *Praeclara narratione.*   16
7. Nahuatl equivalents of numbers, months, and days, LÓPEZ DE GÓMARA, *La conquista de Mexico.*   18
8. Title page, DÍAZ DEL CASTILLO, *Historia verdadera de la conquista de la Nueva España.*   20
9. Title page with portrait of King Charles II, SOLÍS, *Historia de la conquista de México.*   22
10. Ritual battle between Aztec and Tlaxcaltecan warriors, HERRERA Y TORDESILLAS, *Historia general de los hechos de las castellanos.*   24
11. Montezuma carried in a ritual procession, HERRERA Y TORDESILLAS, *Historia general de los hechos de las castellanos.*   25
12. Depictions of Aztec gods and a pyramid, HERRERA Y TORDESILLAS, *Novus Orbis.*   27
13. Ritual dance performed by Aztec nobles and priests, TOVAR, *Historia de la benida de los yndios* (MS).   28
14. Meeting between the Inca, Atahualpa, and Spanish forces at Cajamarca in Peru, XEREZ, *Verdadera relacion de la conquista del Peru.*   34
15. Woodcut of Potosí, CIEZA DE LEÓN, *Parte primera de la chronica del Peru.*   36
16. Title page with the Spanish monarchs' coat of arms, FERNÁNDEZ, *Primera, y segunda parte, de la historia del Peru.*   38
17. Title page portraying the great Inca and his wife along with scenes of a religious procession and sun worship, GARCILASO DE LA VEGA, *Le commentaire royal, ou l'histoire des Yncas.*   40
18. Title page, LÓPEZ DE COGOLLUDO, *Historia de Yucathan.*   45
19. Title page with portraits of pre-Hispanic rulers, a high priest, and scenes from the wars

## LIST OF ILLUSTRATIONS

      of conquest, FERNÁNDEZ DE PIEDRAHITA, *Historia general de las conquistas del nuevo reyno de Granada.*    46

20. Map of Chile, OVALLE, *Historica relacion del reyno de Chile.*    48

21. Chilean Indians playing the ball game "chueca," OVALLE, *Historica relacion del reyno de Chile.*    49

22. Engravings of the coast of southern Chile, SARMIENTO DE GAMBOA, *Viage al Estrecho de Magallanes.*    50

23. First printed image of a buffalo, LÓPEZ DE GÓMARA, *La istoria de las Indias.*    54

24. Portrayal of torture of Indians by Spanish colonists in America, LAS CASAS, *Den Spieghel der Spaense tyrannye.*    55

25. Title page with portraits of pre-Hispanic Inca rulers, HERRERA Y TORDESILLAS, *Historia general de los hechos de los castellanos.*    58

26. Conquistador in symbolic pose with motto below, VARGAS MACHUCA, *Milicia y descripcion de las Indias.*    60

27. Title page with King Philip IV flanked by representations of Spain and America, SOLÓRZANO PEREIRA, *Disputationem de Indiarum jure.*    61

28. Title page depicting a Franciscan friar teaching Mexican Indians, TORQUEMADA, *Monarchia yndiana.*    65

29. Storiated title page of Dominican friars in Peru, MELÉNDEZ, *Tesoros verdaderos de las Yndias.*    67

30. Dominican convent in Lima, Peru, MELÉNDEZ, *Tesoros verdaderos de las Yndias.*    68

31. Title page, CALANCHA, *Coronica moralizada del orden de San Augustin en el Peru.*    69

32. Martyrdom of Fr. Diego Ortiz, CALANCHA, *Coronica moralizada del orden de San Augustin en el Peru.*    70

33. Title page, COLÓN, *Historie... della vita, & de' fatti dell'ammiraglio D. Christoforo Colombo.*    75

34. Portrait of Governor García Hurtado de Mendoza, OVALLE, *Historica relacion.*    76

35. Portrait of Pedro de Oña, *Arauco domado.*    79

36. Stanzas of a poem to be read both as Latin and Spanish, VALDÉS, *Poema heroyco hispano-latino panegyrico.*    80

37. Portrait of Hernán Cortés at sixty-three, LASSO DE LA VEGA, *Cortés valeroso, y Mexicana.*    82

38. Title page, FLORES, *Obra nuevamente compuesta.*    83

39. Portrait of Juan de Castellanos facing his text, *Elegías de varones illustres de Indias.*    85

40. Title page with female figures representing the four continents, CUBERO SEBASTIÁN, *Peregrinacion del mundo.*    87

# PREFACE

THE SPANISH EMPIRE in America, more so than the English empire later, was essentially a projection of the monarchy. In the midst of thousands of private and individual exploitive ventures, the Spanish crown sought and achieved a remarkable degree of centralized bureaucratic control.

It has always been a matter of wonder and admiration that in the sixteenth century the Spanish (or any European country for that matter) were able to organize and maintain the necessary apparatus at home and abroad for hierarchical administrative and financial governance of their immense American colonies. All of this was achieved materially by way of ships and mules and horses, and legally and spiritually by hand-carried pieces of paper. It has been well said that Spanish America was connected to Spain by a bridge of paper.

A significant portion of that paper was, of course, official reports, the conveying of information in narrative form to superiors, sent home from the soldiers and the priests, the judges and clerks and petty officials; and sometimes these reports, when they were not themselves already, by most measures, works of contemporary history, were assembled and digested by others into what were unmistakably full scale histories.

The impulses behind historical writing may be many, beginning with the autobiographical and the genealogical, and extending to the urge of the poet to recount in epic form wondrous events that must be remembered. History is written to do justice to those long dead, whether with condemnation or praise, and to record for posterity the way it really was. One history invariably calls forth another written from a different perspective.

Moreover, in the aftermath of the European arrival in what to the voyagers was a new world, it was necessary also somehow to fit the history of the Americas—in particular the pre-Columbian story of the Indians—into the Judaeo-Christian universal history of mankind, beginning with the first parents, Adam and Eve.

The field and the opportunity presented to the Spanish for writing history in the wake of the great encounter of 1492 was enormous and came just at the moment of maximum fascination in Europe with the literary achievements of the famous Classical historians, many of whom, as it happened, had grappled with subjects that paralleled those about which the Spanish were compelled to write: Xenophon's march to the sea; Caesar's conquest of Gaul; Tacitus on the German tribes.

There is no better way in 1992 to honor the Spanish, we are convinced, than to call attention to their early histories of the Americas, which were, taken together, vast in scope, often original, irreplaceable for the natural and the ethnographic information they have preserved, and sometimes, as in the instance of Bartolomé de las Casas, immortal pleas for justice among men. For grappling with fundamental issues of law, religion, anthropology, and political status, few other bodies of literature within a concentrated period of time are the equal of this Spanish output from the sixteenth and seventeenth centuries. Yet it is apparent that this literature has not received the recognition it deserves as a whole.

No other institution in the United States may be so rich in these first chronicles of the Americas as is the John Carter Brown Library, where one may find, to take a single example, editions of López de Gómara's *La istoria de las Indias* (Saragossa, 1552), in Italian (Rome, 1556), French (Paris, 1569), English (Paris, 1578), and Turkish (Constantinople, 1730). It was logical, therefore, for the Library to undertake, on the occasion of the five hundredth anniversary of the Spanish encounter with the Americas, the preparation of an exhibition and an accompanying catalogue devoted to this important subject.

Professor Angel Delgado-Gomez of the University of Notre Dame had been a National Endowment for the Humanities Fellow at the John Carter Brown Library in 1986–1987, preparing a critical edition of Hernán Cortés's famous five reports on the conquest of Mexico. Sometime after that initial acquaintance, the Library approached Professor Delgado about preparing the present exhibition, in time for 1992. He has done this work splendidly, and the Library is proud of this book, which we anticipate will be received with keen appreciation everywhere in the world where there is an interest in Spanish culture.

Professor Delgado had the great benefit of assistance from the Library's Chief of Cataloguing, Ms. Susan L. Newbury, who provided the rigorous bibliographical structure for Professor Delgado's work and extended it through the year 1800. Ms. Newbury's contribution is particularly revealing of the wide dispersion many of these Spanish histories had throughout Europe, judging from what is found in the JCB collection alone.

Seed money for this project came initially from the Program for Cultural Cooperation between Spain's Ministry of Culture and United States' Universities, which was followed by a larger grant from the Comité Conjunto Hispano-Norteamericano para la Cooperación Cultural y Educativa in Madrid, facilitated by Thomas Middleton, Deputy Executive Director. We are grateful for this support, and also for generous grants at an early stage of the work from Amtraco L. P., headed by Mr. Ricardo Jove, and from the Consul General of Spain in Boston, Mr. Julio Jacoiste. Both Mr. Jove and Mr. Jacoiste have been invaluable friends to the project. A major subsidy for printing and binding was awarded to the Library by the Fundación Ramón Areces. In connection with this grant we wish to thank in particular Sr. Eustasio Rodríguez Alvarez for his advocacy. We wish to acknowledge, also, the interest and support we have received from Ms. Aimée Metzner and Mr. Rafael Mazarrasa of the Spain '92 Foundation, and from Professor José Amor y Vázquez, Professor Emeritus of Hispanic Studies at Brown University, who has been a close advisor from start to finish.

There is no denying that the arrival of Europeans in the Americas, after thousands of years of isolation in the case of both sides at the fateful meeting in 1492, had fearful and tragic consequences. Whatever we can know and understand of this tragedy, however, has come to us primarily through the dedication to truth and understanding of Spanish writers, or indigenous writers trained by the Spanish. Such a level or degree of civilization, expressed in the passion for recording accurately for posterity what happened, and in the capacity for wonder and admiration that is converted into great literature, should never be taken for granted.

NORMAN FIERING,
*Director & Librarian,*
*John Carter Brown Library*

# ACKNOWLEDGMENTS

I WISH TO EXPRESS my sincere gratitude to the staff of the John Carter Brown Library. Preparation of this catalogue would not have been possible without their expertise and most generous support. Special thanks are due to Susan Danforth, who offered valuable ideas towards the format of the exhibit; to Susan Newbury, who prepared the excellent Bibliographical Supplement to this text; and to Richard Hurley, who contributed with his beautiful photographs. I also benefited greatly from the comments and suggestions of Professors Rolena Adorno of Princeton University, José Amor y Vázquez of Brown University, Roberto González Echeverría of Yale University, and Enrique Pupo-Walker of Vanderbilt University. My sincere gratitude to all of them.

This exhibit is dedicated to Don Luis Arocena, professor emeritus of the University of Texas, whose memorable lectures initiated me in this field. It is to be hoped that at least some of his great enthusiasm for the knowledge of matters concerning the New World has been conveyed here.

SPANISH HISTORICAL
WRITING ABOUT THE NEW WORLD
1493–1700

FRONTISPIECE: Pedro de Cieza de León. *La prima parte dell'istorie del Peru.* Venice, 1557. Map of America.

# INTRODUCTION

> No greater misfortune could possibly befall a people than to lack a historian properly to set down their annals; one who with faithful zeal will guard, treasure, and perpetuate all those human events which if left to the frail memory of man and to the mercy of the passing years, will be sacrified upon the altars of time.
>
> —GASPAR DE VILLAGRÁ
> Prologue to *History of New Mexico* (1610)

THE EUROPEAN DISCOVERY of the New World dramatically changed the course of Spanish history. It also opened a vast new field for Spanish historical writing. The modern development of historiography as a social science had its beginnings in the Renaissance. The chronicles of the early Middle Ages amounted to little more than chronological lists of kings and facts in which no analysis of the causes and effects of political, military, and religious life can be found. A concern for the national or secular explanation of events was incorporated in the writing of history for the first time by the Florentine Humanist Leonardo Bruni, who thus revived the Greco-Latin intellectual tradition. Spain's close contacts with Italy—the kingdom of Aragon had long included the southern part of the Italian peninsula—allowed her to participate in that tradition already in the fifteenth century, when a number of histories recorded the last stages of the Reconquest war against the Moors and the efforts by Castile and Aragon to unify the various kingdoms of the Iberian peninsula under one monarchy.

Early Spanish historical writing about the discovery and conquest of the New World made special demands upon authors. First of all, because European readers were unfamiliar with the setting, it was necessary for historians to provide full geographical descriptions of the new territories. Secondly, these early histories necessarily had to deal not only with the enterprises of the Spaniards and their encounters with the natives, but also with the present characteristics and eventually the pasts of the non-European civilizations encountered in the Americas. These two requirements posed a major challenge for historians, for which the newly revived authors of ancient Greece and Rome, who did not even know about the existence of the New World, could not be of much help. Worse yet, the Bible also contained no helpful precedents for dealing with such problems. Thus, the historiographical tradition begun in 1492 had to fill an unparalleled void by a painful process of acquiring knowledge. Historical writing developed from mere descriptions of the aspect and customs of New World peoples to an analysis that could ultimately answer in a satisfactory way the central questions posed by the discovery: Who were these newly found people and how are they related to the inhabitants of the Old World?

Inevitably, the Spanish historian's point of view was Eurocentric, and as a result, his view of both the physical and the human landscape was limited by his beliefs, traditions, and cultural environment, and frequently tainted by social and religious prejudice. Still, the late eighteenth-century German naturalist and explorer Alexander von Humboldt, arguably the first person to study the fauna, flora, and peoples of the Americas in a modern, systematic way, expressed his astonishment at the large amount of accurate observations valuable to later scholars and scientists that had already been accumulated. It also must be noted that the variety of cultural perspectives displayed by historians was significantly enriched after some mestizos and Indians adopted the craft of historian. Their works brought about a reassessment of the values and the ideas of the people who had conquered and settled the continent. The legacy of Spanish historical writing has been fairly synthesized by professor A. Curtis Wilgus with these words: "It will not be surprising that some records and accounts by these men—there were no women—were inaccurate, inexact, prejudiced, imaginative, mystical, metaphysical or downright fictitious. On the whole, nevertheless, the histories were honest, realistic, valuable, even though many cannot meet today's standards of historical probity."

To understand fully the implications of the role of historiography in European thought one must point out that in the sixteenth century the division of knowledge into the modern disciplines and fields had not yet taken place. History included areas now seen as part of the natural sciences, such as biology, botany, and zoology, commonly referred to as natural history, as well as areas now included in the social sciences such as sociology, ethnography, and anthropology, which pertained to the realm of moral (also called general) history. Because of the breadth of "history" in this period, the contribution of Spanish historiography of the New World to the intellectual history of the West can hardly be overstated, although it has not been widely recognized. European historiography was enriched by this new body of literature that contained the earliest descriptions of the physical and human landscape of the New World. While this wealth of information provided fundamental data for the development of other established areas of knowledge such as linguistics, political theory, biology, medicine, and agriculture, it also led to the creation of new ones. The extensive discussions in Spain about the nature of human behavior, stimulated by the encounter with the Indians, were a major contribution to the development of anthropology as an independent social science. Disputes over the conflicting rights of natives and invaders also provided Francisco de Vitoria with the materials to lay the foundations of international law.

The special set of circumstances under which the process of historical writing was accomplished produced important changes in the role of the historian as well as in the characteristics of the text itself. The ideal historian of the Renaissance was a Humanist who, detached from the facts he narrated, ordered and analyzed his sources in a way similar to the modern scholar. Circumstances were different in the first two centuries of colonial life, however; so our approach to the subject of historical discourse must necessarily embrace a much broader definition of that genre. Although not a few of the historians of the New World were true scholars, many of the writings we must consider were produced by authors who do not belong in that select category, but who were, instead, military, civilian, or religious officers directly involved with the facts they described. Sometimes these narrators were simple soldiers (*soldados cronistas*) who recounted the campaigns of discovery and conquest in which they had participated. Fully aware that they did not always possess the necessary training to write history in the learned fashion, they tended to compensate for their lack of formal education by expressing the simple truth, strongly reassured by their having been direct witnesses of the facts they narrated. In another category of non-learned historical discourses were works that were originally legal documents, such as letters, official reports (*relaciones*), or depositions required by the crown in fulfillment of its need to be informed about recent events. These writings were not meant to be formal histories, nor did their authors consider themselves historians, although we may now ascribe to these works the title of histories because of their meaningful contribution to the elucidation of the past or because of their precious value as the first narratives of important events.

Naturally, the considerations that we are presenting here affect in a major way both the tone and the perspective of the texts. Historians throughout the ages have had a number of intentions—praise of individual or collective heroism, expressions of faith, justifications for authority and particular institutions—and all of these appear in rich variety in the Spanish works of our period. That these authors were often directly involved with the events reported often led to subjective assessments, and their texts may contain very personal statements about the political, military, religious, and legal aspects of the Spanish presence in the New World. Furthermore, the encounter with America raised a great number of controversial issues that were very much alive when the historian took up his pen. The interpretation of the past thus led not infrequently to direct calls for future official action concerning the events described. By approving or condemning past behavior historians were often seeking to modify official current policy, or perhaps were hoping to obtain compensation for services rendered to the monarchy, services made explicit in the text. This editorial content is a distinctive characteristic of the New World historical discourse of the time.

It is easy for us, five hundred years after Columbus's landing on a Caribbean island, to comprehend the immense consequences of that encounter between peoples who until then had remained isolated from each other. But, as professor J. H. Elliott has noted, we must bear in mind that Europeans took a very long time to understand the consequences of the exploration and European colonization of the New World. The case of great minds of that time, like Erasmus or Cervantes, who remained largely indifferent to the discovery, reflected a prevalent attitude rather than an exception. Following the invention of the modern techniques of printing in the mid-fifteenth century, Europeans were being flooded with a spurious literature of imaginary travels and chivalric romances that freely mixed fact and fiction while at the same time reassuring the reader of their true content. In such a cultural context, it is not surprising that historians reporting on America tended to be overly insistent about the truth of their accounts and to overstate the importance of their observations and narratives, for they had to promote that cause among readers who could quickly dismiss these writings as grossly exaggerated facts and even mere fiction. We may easily agree with Francisco López de Gómara's famous claim that the discovery of the Indies was the most important event of human history after the incarnation of Jesus Christ, but I find no evidence that such a belief was shared by anyone else at that time.

The list of actually published Spanish books on the New World is certainly a long one. But even so, a number of relevant works, including some masterpieces of the genre, remained in manuscript form until modern times. There are several reasons for this. One of the ways the Spanish crown tried to protect its political and economic interests was through censorship. Since 1502 a royal license issued by the Consejo Real (after 1554, by the Consejo de Indias) was required to allow publication of any book dealing with the Indies, and this resulted in works being banned for publication due to their highly controversial subjects or because the Spanish feared the works would give away classified information. In other cases, publication was not possible for lack of a financial sponsor. Finally, we must take into account that many works of historiographical value were not intended for publication at the time they were written. This rather large group includes most of the *relaciones* by conquistadors as well as documented ethnographic studies by churchmen which circulated internally within their religious orders.

This exhibit aims to show the rich variety of Spanish historiographical works produced in Spain and her colonies during the first two hundred years of her involvement with the New World. Making a narrow selection out of such a vast field necessarily requires a balance between the various groups of books to be considered, and regrettably not every work that scholars deem valuable may be included. I have given preference naturally to titles published before 1700, but a few important ones that were published later have been included as well. The exhibit is arranged thematically, but also follows a chronological order of events whenever possible.

For the preparation of this text many works were consulted, and it is impossible to give due individual recognition to the source of each idea and fact. A list of the works often consulted is provided in the bibliography. Among them the two most important sources are F. Esteve Barba's *Historiografía Indiana* and A. Curtis Wilgus's *The Historiography of Latin America*.

# I · *Novus Orbis: The Early Accounts*

THE EUROPEAN DISCOVERY of the New World was both intended and accidental. Columbus, an experienced Genoese merchant sailor with a penchant for learned books, had conceived a plan to sail to the East by heading west. This idea was based on an old assumption dating as far back as the Greek geographer Ptolemy, who believed that the world was round and that the distance between Europe's far west and the Orient's far east was small. This notion found new life in the Renaissance in the writings of Pierre d'Ailly and Paolo dal Pozzo Toscanelli, authors well known to Columbus, and in the late fifteenth century it acquired a new economic dimension.

The Portuguese had made progress in establishing a sea route that would give them direct access to the increasingly profitable spice trade with the Orient, but the trip around the southern tip of Africa proved long and risky. Columbus's plan to sail directly westward was offered to the king of Portugal as a faster and less expensive alternative, but neither he nor the French and English monarchs, whom he also approached, were convinced of its feasibility. Only Queen Isabella listened and, after some hesitation, agreed to sponsor Columbus's enterprise. Columbus, promised by Her Majesty the new title of Admiral of the Ocean Sea, left Palos, a fishing village in Southern Spain, with a small fleet of three caravels on the 3rd of August, 1492.

The trip was a momentous one. Spain had only recently achieved some degree of political unity by virtue of the marriage between Ferdinand of Aragon and Isabella of Castile, and the country had also just completed a long campaign to expel the infidel Moors from Iberian soil by conquering the kingdom of Granada, the last Muslim bastion in the peninsula. The discovery of new lands on October 12th provided the Catholic Kings, Ferdinand and Isabella, with an opportunity for territorial expansion overseas. Furthermore, following a belief well established in the Europe of that time—also shared by the pilgrims of the *Mayflower*—Spaniards thought that their enterprise obeyed a providential design, a belief that the Pope sanctioned at the highest level by conferring upon it the character of a Christian crusade.

Spanish intervention across the ocean purportedly served a triple interest: God, the crown, and private wealth, all three neatly conceived as mutually complementary. From its very beginning, then, the rapid process of discovery, conquest, and colonization that was to take place was guided by the three corresponding agents of those goals: the Church, which took responsibility for its missionary aspects; the king and his growing body of bureaucrats, who exerted administrative control over the territories overseas; and finally the adventurous sailors, soldiers, and merchants who risked their lives for the pursuit of glory and wealth.

But were they new lands at all? Not so, according to Columbus, who had stumbled into some islands which he thought must be located near Cipango (Japan) or the east coast of Cathay (China). It is indeed one of the great ironies of the world's history that the European discoverer of the "New" World (new to Europeans) never quite acknowledged the full extent of his deed, for this would have implied a gross mistake in his estimate of the distance between Spain and Japan. Columbus, who sailed three more times across the ocean and even saw the continental coastline of Central and South America, apparently still believed when he died in 1506 that the lands he had discovered belonged to Asia, and he accordingly named them the Indies.

The earliest historiography of the New World is mostly descriptive and consists largely of reports of sea travels by witnesses. Landscapes are only vaguely described, although with awe and even allusions to Paradise or mythical places. As for the islanders, authors can only reflect on their brief encounters with them marred by a frustrating language problem. Still, in just a few years an image of the New World as a distinct geographical entity slowly emerged.

1. *Christopher Columbus.* EPISTOLA. [Rome, 1493].

This is the first publication on the New World. Columbus (1451–1506) presumably wrote this *Letter* to Luis de Santángel aboard the *Niña* on his return trip so as to officially proclaim his discovery, and in consequence its tone is exalted. In summarizing what he saw, Columbus displayed a characteristic mixture of accurate observations with fantastic hypotheses, many of them rooted in his certainty that he was in Asia. He described the Taino Indians as a people of Biblical innocence, naked in their bodies and incapable of any wrongdoing. Their island, which he named Hispaniola, is vaguely depicted as a true paradise of lush green vegetation and balmy weather. Columbus also made reference to the cannibals, people he had not seen but of whom he had heard said that they customarily raided the islands inhabited by peaceful people in order to enslave the women and kill the men, whose flesh they ate. The original purpose of the trip had not been realized, since neither gold nor spices were found, but the founding of Navidad, the first European colony in the New World, is described as a promising start. The letter ends with an enthusiastic affirmation of both future wealth and the great spiritual benefit for Christianity that will result from the unproblematic conversion of the natives.

Columbus's *Carta* was published in its original Spanish in Barcelona, in April of 1493. Nine editions of a Latin translation by Leandro (Aliander) de Cosco, entitled *Epistola*, quickly appeared in Rome, Paris, Antwerp, and Basel. Although just a brief document, Columbus's *Letter* had a major influence on the early European concept of the New World.

FIGURE 1. Christopher Columbus. *Epistola*. Basel, 1493. This is the first printed illustration attempting to show Columbus's "discovery" of the "Indies." The two groups of Indians shown react differently to the arrival of the Europeans: one flees in panic; the other engages in an exchange of gifts (Enlarged).

2. *Diego Alvarez Chanca.* RELACIÓN. Madrid, 1825.

Dr. Chanca was the appointed physician on Columbus's second expedition to the new islands, which sailed from Spain in 1493. He wrote this remarkably objective and accurate report for the Seville city council upon his return to Spain in 1494. Among other things he narrated the expedition's one-week visit to the island of Guadeloupe. Because the native men on the island had left to raid another island, he had an opportunity to see their towns undisturbed. Shocking evidence of their cannibalistic practices is given without making any judgments. Chanca gives details about the flora and fauna of several islands including Hispaniola, which he found a mixed case of beautiful vegetation and unhealthy humidity. His view of the natives was necessarily less naïve than Columbus's previous one, for by the time this account was written the Indians had rebelled against the settlers of Navidad leaving no survivors. But Chanca nonetheless shows little prejudice and provides instead valuable information about local customs and produce.

Alvarez Chanca's report was known to some of his contemporaries, but it remained unpublished until Martín Fernández de Navarrete included it in his *Collection of Spanish sea-travels since the fifteenth century*, published in Spain in the nineteenth century.


3. *Pietro Martire d'Anghiera.* DE ORBE NOVO DECADES. Alcalá de Henares, 1516.

Peter Martyr (1457–1526), known in Spain as Pedro Mártir de Anglería, was born Pietro Martire d'Anghiera in Lombardy, Italy. He moved to Spain in 1487 and remained there the rest of his life, serving the Spanish court first as a soldier and, after becoming a priest, as a courtier, chaplain, teacher, and ambassador. Martyr, a learned Humanist, was an early enthusiast of the New World and its first major historian. In 1520 he became secretary to the Council of the Indies and later was appointed by emperor Charles V as the first official chronicler of the Indies. Although Martyr never set foot in the New World, he used his privileged position as a courtier to gather a great wealth of information from documents and through personal interviews. Following the model of the Latin historian Titus Livius, the *Decades* are volumes written in Latin divided into ten books each. They cover all aspects of the New World—the geography, the natural world (he was the first to describe minerals, plants and animals in detail), the natives, and all major events after the discovery. Martyr was the first to establish a connection between the New World and Classical antiquity. He compared the peaceful Caribbean islanders with the happy inhabitants of the Golden Age, and thought that myths like the Amazons, mermaids, and the fountain of eternal youth could be located across the ocean.

Martyr went on to write five more *Decades*, in addition to the three in this edition. The complete set of eight was published posthumously, also in Alcalá de Henares, in 1530. His

FIGURE 2. Martín Fernández de Enciso. *Suma de geographia*. Seville, 1519. The first practical guide to sailing in American waters but "contemporary" history as well.

influence was pervasive throughout Europe. An English translation of the first four decades by Richard Eden, published under the title *The decades of the Newe World or West India*, was part of the first English book dealing with the New World, published in London in 1555.

4. *Amerigo Vespucci.* MUNDUS NOVUS. [Paris, 1503].

Vespucci (1451–1512) was a merchant from Florence who moved to Seville in 1492. He quickly became interested in the early discoveries and apparently participated in some of them, since he eventually received the royal appointment of *piloto mayor*. The exact details of his travels are the subject of a long controversy among scholars, who have argued bitterly about the authenticity of his writings. However, it seems undisputable that *Mundus Novus* is a remake in Latin of a letter written in Italian by Vespucci. The anonymous editor added a few spicy and ficticious comments to an original text already full of exaggerations and inconsistencies. The people of the New World are described as a friendly group of noble savages who spend their happy lives making love and eating human flesh. Although very little precise geographic information is given, *Mundus Novus* is credited with being the first printed text that identifies the New World as a new distinct continent, which by a strange train of circumstances was later named after him instead of Columbus.

The popularity of *Mundus Novus* outside of Spain was immense. In the five years following the first printing, twenty editions appeared in Europe, seven in Germany alone.

5. *Martín Fernández de Enciso.* SUMA DE GEOGRAPHIA QUE TRATA DE TODAS LAS PARTIDAS Y PROVINCIAS DEL MUNDO: EN ESPECIAL DE LAS INDIAS.
Seville, 1519.

Fernández de Enciso (*c.* 1470–*c.* 1528) was one of the earliest settlers in Santo Domingo, the capital of Hispaniola, where he practiced law and participated actively in sea expeditions. In 1514 he served with Pedro Arias de Avila (known as Pedrarias), the first governor of Castilla del Oro (Panama), and upon his return to Spain, he wrote the *Suma*. As its long title indicates, his work attempts to cover the world's geography, but its most valuable information is the chapter on the West Indies. The word "America" was here used for the first time in a Spanish printed text, a denomination that in Spain remained rare until the nineteenth-century—the word "Indies" being preferred. Using a great variety of both oral and written sources plus his own experience, Enciso compiled a practical book with useful information, especially for pilots. In his descriptions of the natives he gives precise information about the distinct physical characteristics of each tribe as well as their particular attitude towards the Spanish.

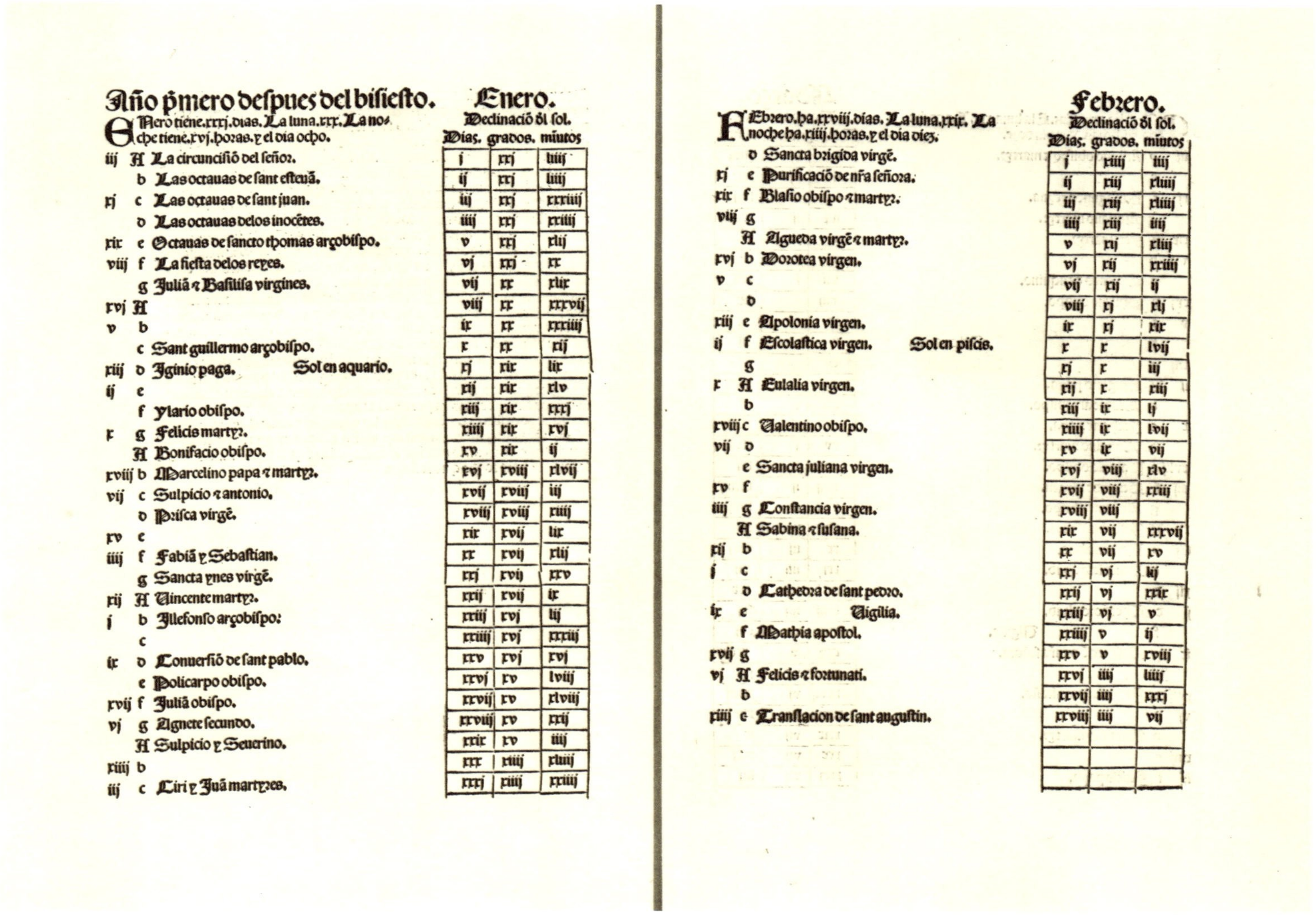

# Año p̃mero despues del bisiesto. Enero.

Enero tiene.xxxj.dias. La luna.xxx. La noche tiene.xvj.horas.y el dia ocho.

| | | | Declinació dl sol. Dias. | grados. | minutos |
|---|---|---|---|---|---|
| iij | A | La circuncisiõ del señor. | j | xxj | liiij |
| | b | Las octauas de sant esteuã. | ij | xxj | liiij |
| xj | c | Las octauas de sant juan. | iij | xxj | xxxiiij |
| | d | Las octauas delos inocẽtes. | iiij | xxj | xxiiij |
| xix | e | Octauas de sancto thomas arçobispo. | v | xxj | xlij |
| viij | f | La fiesta delos reyes. | vj | xxj | xx |
| | g | Juliã ⁊ Basilisa virgines. | vij | xx | xlix |
| xvj | A | | viij | xx | xxxvij |
| v | b | | ix | xx | xxxiiij |
| | c | Sant guillermo arçobispo. | x | xx | xij |
| xiij | d | Iginio papa. Sol en aquario. | xj | xix | lix |
| ij | e | | xij | xix | xlv |
| | f | Ylario obispo. | xiij | xix | xxxj |
| x | g | Felicis martyr. | xiiij | xix | xvj |
| | A | Bonifacio obispo. | xv | xix | ij |
| xviij | b | Marcelino papa ⁊ martyr. | xvj | xviij | xlvij |
| vij | c | Sulpicio ⁊ antonio. | xvij | xviij | iij |
| | d | Prisca virgẽ. | xviij | xviij | xiiij |
| xv | e | | xix | xvij | lix |
| iiij | f | Fabiã y Sebastian. | xx | xvij | xlij |
| | g | Sancta ynes virgẽ. | xxj | xvij | xxv |
| xij | A | Vincente martyr. | xxij | xvij | ix |
| j | b | Illefonso arçobispo. | xxiij | xvj | lij |
| | c | | xxiiij | xvj | xxxiij |
| ix | d | Conuersiõ de sant pablo. | xxv | xvj | xvj |
| | e | Policarpo obispo. | xxvj | xv | lviij |
| xvij | f | Juliã obispo. | xxvij | xv | xlviij |
| vj | g | Agnete secundo. | xxviij | xv | xxij |
| | A | Sulpicio y Seuerino. | xxix | xv | iiij |
| xiiij | b | | xxx | xiiij | xliiij |
| iij | c | Ciri y Juã martyres. | xxxj | xiiij | xxiiij |

# Febrero.

Febrero.ha.xxviij.dias. La luna.xxix. La noche ha.xiiij.horas.y el dia diez.

| | | | Declinació dl sol. Dias. | grados. | minutos |
|---|---|---|---|---|---|
| | d | Sancta brigida virgẽ. | j | xiiij | iiij |
| xj | e | Purificació de nr̃a señora. | ij | xiij | xliiij |
| xix | f | Blasio obispo ⁊ martyr. | iij | xiij | xliiij |
| viij | g | | iiij | xiij | iiij |
| | A | Agueda virgẽ ⁊ martyr. | v | xij | xliij |
| xvj | b | Dorotea virgen. | vj | xij | xxiiij |
| v | c | | vij | xij | ij |
| | d | | viij | xj | xlj |
| xiij | e | Apolonia virgen. | ix | xj | xix |
| ij | f | Escolastica virgen. Sol en piscis. | x | x | lvij |
| | g | | xj | x | iij |
| x | A | Eulalia virgen. | xij | x | xiij |
| | b | | xiij | ix | lj |
| xviij | c | Valentino obispo. | xiiij | ix | lvij |
| vij | d | | xv | ix | vij |
| | e | Sancta juliana virgen. | xvj | viij | xlv |
| xv | f | | xvij | viij | xxiij |
| iiij | g | Constancia virgen. | xviij | viij | |
| | A | Sabina ⁊ susana. | xix | vij | xxxvij |
| xij | b | | xx | vij | xv |
| j | c | | xxj | vj | lij |
| | d | Cathedra de sant pedro. | xxij | vj | xxix |
| ix | e | Vigilia. | xxiij | vj | v |
| | f | Mathia apostol. | xxiiij | v | ij |
| xvij | g | | xxv | v | xviij |
| vj | A | Felicis ⁊ fortunati. | xxvj | iiij | liiij |
| | b | | xxvij | iiij | xxxj |
| xiiij | c | Translacion de sant augustin. | xxviij | iiij | vij |
| | | | | | |
| | | | | | |
| | | | | | |

FIGURE 3. Martín Fernández de Enciso. *Suma de geographia.* Seville, 1519. The tables show the movements of the sun for each day of the year. Days are identified by number and by the name of the corresponding saint in the Catholic calendar.

The *Suma* seems to have given Enciso a certain celebrity. It was reprinted in 1530 and 1546.

6. *Gonzalo Fernández de Oviedo y Valdés.* DE LA NATURAL HYSTORIA DE LAS INDIAS. Toledo, 1526.

Oviedo (1478–1557) was descended from a noble family and received a formal education. He served in important positions at the royal court and in Italy, where he associated with some illustrious Humanists. In 1512 he traveled to the New World, where he spent most of his life serving as a representative of the crown in various cities. Upon his second return to Spain, in

FIGURE 4. Gonzalo Fernández de Oviedo y Valdés. *De la natural hystoria de las Indias*. Toledo, 1526. This woodcut illustrates Oviedo's description of the Indian method of making fire with two sticks.

FIGURE 5. Gonzalo Fernández de Oviedo y Valdés. *De la natural hystoria de las Indias*. Toledo, 1526. This woodcut illustrates Oviedo's description of an Indian hammock.

1523, Emperor Charles V asked him to write a report on the Indies. Oviedo had carefully taken extensive notes on all aspects of the European "discoveries," but this work, known as the *Sumario*, is only a report quickly written from memory. It is mostly devoted to the natural history of the Indies, which had hitherto been overlooked by authors like Peter Martyr who had never been there—a point stressed by Oviedo himself who resented Martyr's reputation. The author provides new botanical, zoological, and ethnographical information, mostly on the Caribbean islands and the Panama region, but some brief references are also given to administrative matters, the Indians, the gold mines, and the recently found route to the Pacific Spice Islands. Oviedo's down-to-earth and almost journalistic style is in sharp contrast to the enthusiastic tone of astonishment and awe so typical of the early Humanists interested in the New World.

Oviedo's *Sumario* quickly earned him a solid reputation as the best informed person on the New World who had direct knowledge of his subject. He later elaborated most of this material in his voluminous *Historia general* (No. 41).

## II · *Into the Mainland: The Conquest of Mexico*

AFTER SETTLING IN Hispaniola, the Spanish moved to establish colonies on the adjacent islands of Puerto Rico (1508), Jamaica (1509), and Cuba (1512). From their ports frequent expeditions were launched to reconnoiter the continental coast, such as the one from Puerto Rico commanded by Juan Ponce de León, which discovered Florida in 1512. The major goal of all these expeditions remained the search for a passage to the continent of Asia, which many still thought lay close to the newly found islands. Vasco Núñez de Balboa's discovery of the Pacific Ocean in 1513 made a land passage possible, but hardly convenient. The coveted sea passage, however, which the French and the English were also trying to find north of Florida, proved elusive.

Two expeditions launched from Cuba by Governor Diego Velázquez brought news of a different kind: a rich and populated area north of Yucatan ruled by a great lord. A third expedition, consisting of twelve ships and some five hundred Spaniards headed by Hernando Cortés, sailed for Mexico in 1519. Cortés founded the city of Veracruz and, after sinking his ships to prevent retreat, led his men in a long march to Tenochtitlan. Two years later he had secured for his monarch a vast territory, larger and more populated than Spain. The conquest of Mexico in 1521 significantly altered the European perception of the New World. First, the Aztec treasures finally delivered on the much announced but yet unfulfilled promise of riches. Secondly, the peoples of Mexico impressed their conquerors with their high degree of civilization, which in many respects resembled more that of the Christian invaders than of the Caribbean islanders.

The historiography of the conquest of Mexico and the early Spanish colonial period is very rich, encompassing the whole spectrum of works pertaining to the genre. It goes from numerous writings by soldier-chroniclers who witnessed the facts, such as Cortés himself, to the elaborate and well-researched histories of Humanists, and it also includes works by mestizo authors who incorporated in their output the Mexican perspective on the conquest.

7a. *Hernán Cortés.* CARTA DE RELACIÓN. Seville, 1522.

Cortés (1485–1547) sent five long reports (also known as "letters of relation") to Emperor Charles V, detailing his progress in the conquest of Mexico. This is the second one, signed in Segura de la Frontera (Tlaxcala) on the 30th October, 1520. Cortés narrates the wars and alliances that took place on the way to Tenochtitlan, and at the same time provides vivid descriptions of the land and the peoples he encounters. Cortés's ethnographic interest culminates in his splendid description of the great city, its buildings, institutions, and the court of its ruler Montezuma. He frequently compared the Aztec achievements to those of Christian civilization. The latter part of the letter is dedicated to the narration of his successful skirmish with a rival expedition sent by Velázquez, with whom Cortés had broken off, and the Spanish retreat to Tlaxcala after they were expelled from Tenochtitlan by the rebellious Mexicans. Throughout the letter Cortés vindicated his shaky legal position by skillfully laying out the political and religious benefits that might derive from the enterprise he commanded. Cortés no doubt had a good grasp of the political consequences of his enterprise. Fully aware that the territories he intended to subdue were a radically new geographic entity, he created a distinct administrative province for them, called New Spain. This was the first

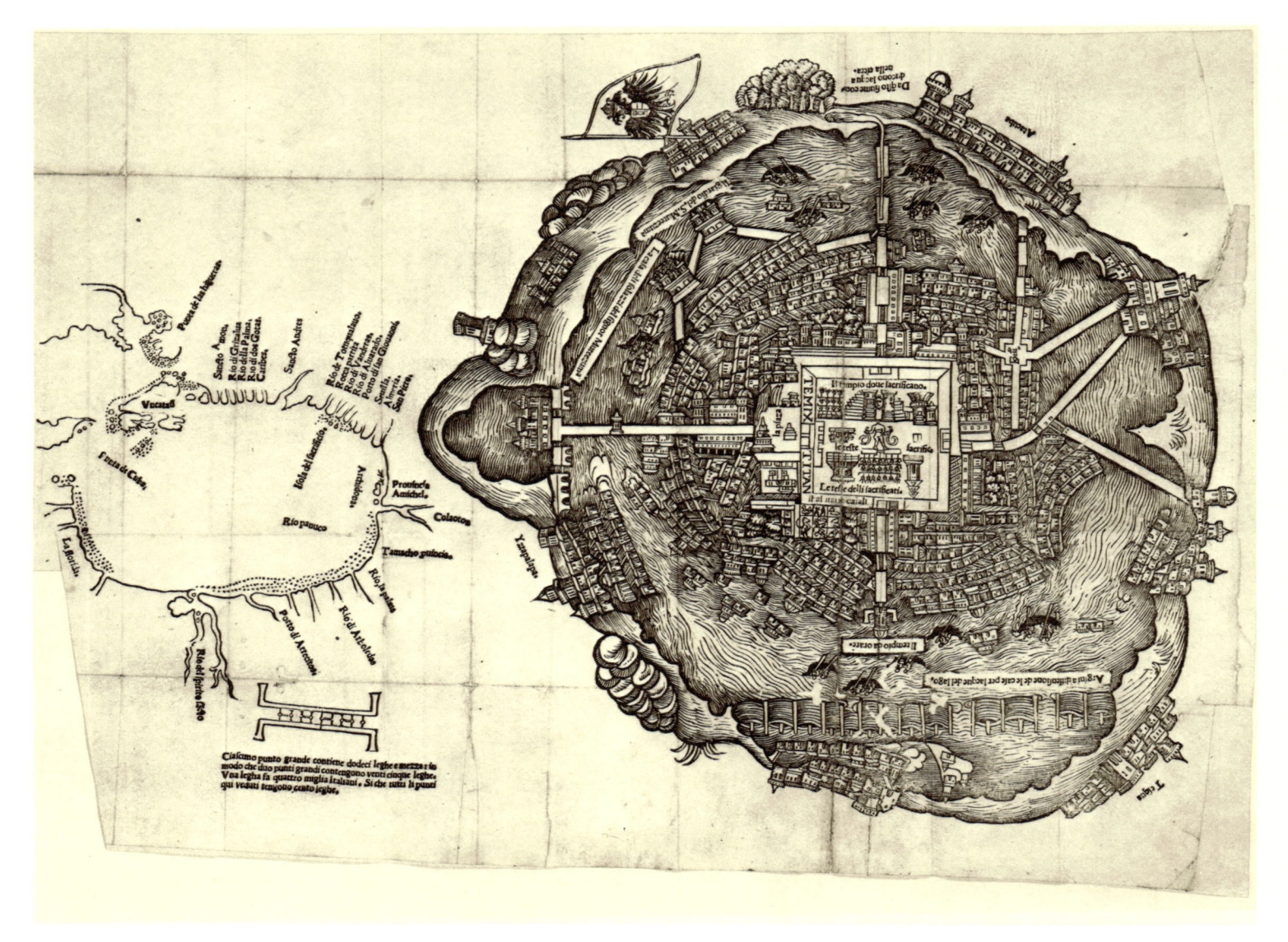

FIGURE 6. Hernán Cortés. *Praeclara narratione*. Venice, 1524. Manuscript versions of this plan of Tenochtitlan and map of the Gulf of Mexico were presumably sent to Spain by Cortés with his second letter to Charles V. The plan of Tenochtitlan (here called Temixtitan) is the first published view of a city in the New World. The Templo Mayor is shown at its center, and the city is linked to other towns around the lake by several causeways. The map of the Gulf of Mexico is remarkably accurate, except that it shows the Yucatan Peninsula as an island.

time the name of a European nation was used with the adjective "new" to name an American territory.

7b. CARTA TERCERA DE RELACIÓN. Seville, 1523.

7c. QUARTA RELACIÓN. Toledo, 1525.

In his third letter, signed in Coyoacan, Mexico, on May 15th, 1522, Cortés narrates his successful siege of Tenochtitlan that concluded the conquest of Mexico, as well as his reorganization of the country under Spanish rule. This includes the founding of cities and the development of agriculture and mining, as well as further land and sea expeditions to the outer limits of New Spain. The fourth letter, signed in Tenochtitlan (later called Mexico City) on October 15, 1524, dwells on the same themes.

These three letters became quickly known in Europe. Fourteen editions in Latin, Italian, and German were published between 1522 and 1532. Ramusio (No. 8) included all three in his volume on the New World. The first and fifth letters remained unpublished until the nineteenth century.

8. RELATIONE DI ALCUNE COSE DELLA NUONA [*sic*] SPAGNA. [Venice, 1556].

A number of the expeditionaries who participated alongside Cortés wrote valuable relations on the conquest of Mexico. The ones authored by Andrés de Tapia and Bernardino Vázquez de Tapia were mainly legal depositions, but others like that of Fr. Francisco de Aguilar were written with a purely historiographical purpose. Ironically, the only writing in this category to be published in the sixteenth century is that by an unidentified soldier usually known as the Anonymous Conqueror. All copies of the original Spanish manuscript were lost, but an Italian translation of his relation appeared in the third volume of *Delle navigatione et viaggi*, a compilation of writings on the New World edited by the Venetian G. B. Ramusio. The author relied on his own observations, but he also knew Cortés's second letter, which he copied in some instances. The relation is an interesting ethnographic survey of Mexican life containing both accurate descriptions and incorrect information, although it is very likely that the latter was in great part added by the translator.

9. *Francisco López de Gómara*. LA ISTORIA DE LAS INDIAS. Y CONQUISTA DE MEXICO. Saragossa, 1552.

López de Gómara (1511–1564) was a priest with solid Humanistic training. He served in Spain and Italy as a cleric, and after meeting Hernando Cortés in Spain, became his chaplain and was commissioned to write a history of the conquest of Mexico. Gómara never went to the New World, but Cortés supplied him with abundant oral and written documentation regarding New Spain. His exact rendering of many Nahuatl terms and their meanings is also evidence that he had access to other sources. Following the Classical tradition he knew well, Gómara, a gifted writer, conceived of his book as a heroic tale the structure of which was provided by the biography of Cortés. Gómara's sustained tone of admiration and his frequent use of eloquent speeches were intended to underline his view of the Spanish conquest of Mexico as a great personal achievement. Cortés is presented as one of world history's major figures, worthy of emulation and the equal of Alexander the Great and Julius Caesar. The

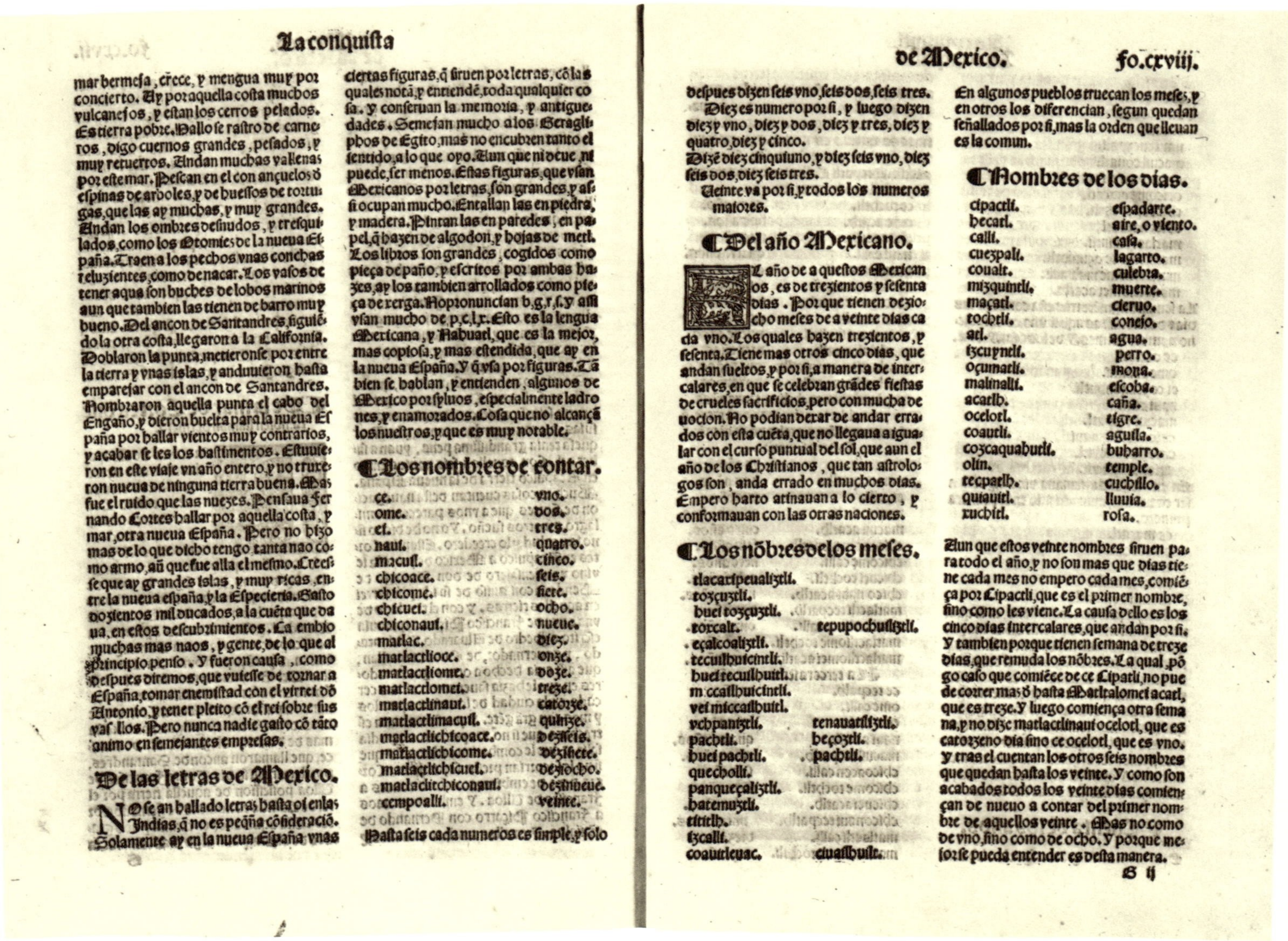

La conquista

mar bermeja, crece, y mengua muy por concierto. Ay por aquella costa muchos vulcanejos, y estan los cerros pelados. Es tierra pobre. Hallose rastro de carneros, digo cuernos grandes, pesados, y muy retuertos. Andan muchas vallenas por este mar. Pescan en el con anzuelos de espinas de arboles, y de huessos de tortugas, que las ay muchas, y muy grandes. Andan los ombres desnudos, y tresquilados, como los Otomies de la nueua España. Traen a los pechos vnas conchas reluzientes, como de nacar. Los vasos de tener agua son buches de lobos marinos aun que tambien las tienen de barro muy bueno. Del ancon de Santandres, siguiẽdo la otra costa, llegaron a la California. Doblaron la punta, metieronse por entre la tierra y vnas islas, y anduuieron hasta emparejar con el ancon de Santandres. Nombraron aquella punta el cabo del Engaño, y dieron buelta para la nueua España por hallar vientos muy contrarios, y acabar se les los bastimentos. Estuuieron en este viaje vn año entero, y no truxeron nueua de ninguna tierra buena. Mas fue el ruido que las nuezes. Pensaua Fernando Cortes hallar por aquella costa, y mar, otra nueua España. Pero no hizo mas de lo que dicho tengo tanta nao como armo, aũ que fue alla el mesmo. Creese que ay grandes islas, y muy ricas, entre la nueua España, y la Especieria. Gasto dozientos mil ducados, a la cuẽta que da, en estos descubrimientos. La embio muchas mas naos, y gente, de lo que al principio penso. Y fueron causa, como despues diremos, que vuiesse de tornar a España, tomar enemistad con el virrey dõ Antonio, y tener pleito cõ el rei sobre sus vasallos. Pero nunca nadie gasto cõ tãto animo en semejantes empresas.

De las letras de Mexico.

No se an hallado letras hasta oi en las Indias, q̃ no es pequẽa cõsideració. Solamente ay en la nueua España vnas ciertas figuras, q̃ siruen por letras, cõ las quales notã, y entiendẽ, toda qualquier cosa. y conseruan la memoria, y antiguedades. Semejan mucho a los Geroglificos de Egito, mas no encubren tanto el sentido, a lo que oyo. Aun que ni deue ni puede, ser menos. Estas figuras, que vsan Mexicanos por letras, son grandes, y assi ocupan mucho. Entallan las en piedra, y madera. Pintan las en paredes, en papel, q̃ hazen de algodon, y hojas de metl. Los libros son grandes, cogidos como pieça de paño, y escritos por ambas hazes, ay los tambien arrollados como pieça de xerga. No pronuncian b, g, r, s, y assi vsan mucho de p, c, l, x. Esto es la lengua Mexicana, y Nahuatl, que es la mejor, mas copiosa, y mas estendida, que ay en la nueua España. Y q̃ vsa por figuras. Tãbien se hablan, y entienden, algunos de Mexico por silvos, especialmente ladrones, y enamorados. Cosa que no alcançã los nuestros, y que es muy notable.

Los nombres de contar.

| | |
|---|---|
| ce. | vno. |
| ome. | dos. |
| ei. | tres. |
| naui. | quatro. |
| macuil. | cinco. |
| chicoace. | seis. |
| chicome. | siete. |
| chicuei. | ocho. |
| chiconaui. | nueue. |
| matlac. | diez. |
| matlactlioce. | onze. |
| matlactliome. | doze. |
| matlactliomei. | treze. |
| matlactlinaui. | catorze. |
| matlactlimacuil. | quinze. |
| matlactlichicoace. | dezi seis. |
| matlactlichicome. | dezisiete. |
| matlactlichicuei. | deziocho. |
| matlactlichiconaui. | dezinueue. |
| cempoalli. | veinte. |

Hasta seis cada numero es simple, y solo

de Mexico. fo.cxviij.

despues dizen seis vno, seis dos, seis tres. Diez es numero por si, y luego dizen diez y vno, diez y dos, diez y tres, diez y quatro, diez y cinco. Dizẽ diez cinquiuno, y diez seis vno, diez seis dos, diez seis tres. Veinte vã por si, y todos los numeros mayores.

Del año Mexicano.

El año de aquestos Mexicanos, es de trezientos y sesenta dias. Por que tienen dezi ocho meses de a veinte dias cada vno. Los quales hazen trezientos y sesenta. Tiene mas otros cinco dias, que andan sueltos, y por si, a manera de intercalares, en que se celebran grãdes fiestas de crueles sacrificios, pero con mucha deuocion. No podian dexar de andar errados con esta cuẽta, que no llegaua a igualar con el curso puntual del sol, que aun el año de los Christianos, que tan astrologos son, anda errado en muchos dias. Empero harto atinauan a lo cierto, y conformauan con las otras naciones.

Los nõbres de los meses.

| | |
|---|---|
| tlacaxipeualiztli. | |
| tozçuztli. | |
| hueitozçuztli. | |
| toxcalt. | tepupochuiliztli. |
| eçalcoaliztli. | |
| tecuilhuicintli. | |
| hueitecuilhuitl. | |
| miccailhuicintli. | |
| veimiccailhuitl. | |
| vchpaniztli. | tenauatiliztli. |
| pachtli. | heçoztli. |
| hueipachtli. | pachtli. |
| quechollí. | |
| panqueçaliztli. | |
| hatemuztli. | |
| tititlh. | |
| izcalli. | |
| coauitleuac. | ciuailhuitl. |

En algunos pueblos truecan los meses, y en otros los diferencian, segun quedan señallados por si, mas la orden que lleuan es la comun.

Nombres de los dias.

| | |
|---|---|
| cipactli. | espadarte. |
| hecatl. | aire, o viento. |
| calli. | casa. |
| cuezpali. | lagarto. |
| coualt. | culebra. |
| mizquintli. | muerte. |
| maçatl. | cieruo. |
| tochtli. | conejo. |
| atl. | agua. |
| izcuyntli. | perro. |
| oçumatli. | mona. |
| malinalli. | escoba. |
| acatlh. | caña. |
| ocelotl. | tigre. |
| coautli. | aguila. |
| cozcaquahutli. | buharro. |
| olin. | temple. |
| tecpatlh. | cuchillo. |
| quiauitl. | lluuia. |
| xuchitl. | rosa. |

Aun que estos veinte nombres siruen para todo el año, y no son mas que dias tiene cada mes no empero cada mes, comiẽça por Cipactli, que es el primer nombre, sino como les viene. La causa dello es los cinco dias intercalares, que andan por si. Y tambien porque tienen semana de treze dias, que remuda los nõbres. La qual, põgo caso que comiẽce de ce Cipatli, no puede correr mas de hasta Matltalomei acatl, que es treze. Y luego comiença otra semana, y no dize matlactlinaui ocelotl, que es catorzeno dia sino ce ocelotl, que es vno. y tras el cuentan los otros seis nombres que quedan hasta los veinte. Y como son acabados todos los veinte dias comiençan de nueuo a contar del primer nombre de aquellos veinte. Mas no como de vno, sino como de ocho. Y porque mejor se pueda entender es desta manera.

B ij

FIGURE 7. Francisco López de Gómara. *La conquista de Mexico.* Saragossa, 1552. In his discussion of Mexican culture, Gómara provides the Nahuatl equivalents of numbers one to twenty, the names of the eighteen months in the Aztec calendar, and the individual names of the twenty days contained in each month.

book also has numerous ethnographic chapters on the indigenous people of Mexico and their customs prior to the conquest in which, like Cortés, he frequently praises their skill but abhors their religious practices.

Gómara's book was published as the second part of his *Istoria de las Indias* (No. 42). It became extremely popular in Europe, with early editions in Italian (1556) and French (1568). An English translation of the second part was published in London in 1578 under the title *The pleasant historie of the conquest of the Weast India now called New Spain.*

10. *Bernal Díaz del Castillo.* HISTORIA VERDADERA DE LA CONQUISTA DE LA NUEVA ESPAÑA. Madrid, [1632].

Díaz del Castillo (1496–1584) participated as a soldier in the conquest of Mexico under Cortés and then in other military campaigns, before settling in Guatemala where he lived a long life. Unlike other famous conquistadors, Díaz never distinguished himself in his military career. His fame rests solely on his book. His initial intention might have been to write a relation designed to inform the royal officials of his service to the Crown, but upon reading Gómara's book (No. 9), he enlarged it into a comprehensive history. No less than Gómara, Díaz admired Cortés, but his book intends to portray the conquest of Mexico as a collective rather than an individual effort. Díaz was fully aware of his technical inability as an historian, since, unlike Gómara, he did not have the training to write in the appropriately high literary style. But he believed his witnessing of the facts more than compensated for his poor rhetorical skills. Endowed with a prodigious memory—he started his work when he was in his seventies—Díaz identified the names of all persons and places of the conquest. He provided memorable descriptions of Tenochtitlan, and lively portraits of Cortés, Alvarado, Montezuma, Cuauhtemoc, and many others. His account is also enriched with innumerable personal anecdotes not recorded anywhere else. His major success lies in his ability to recreate and evaluate his own perceptions and feelings as a conquistador, which he conveys in a sincere and almost conversational style.

The *Historia verdadera* was published long after Díaz's death by Fr. Alonso Remón, a Mercedarian who edited the text so as to praise his order. In the last two centuries it has become one of the most popular books on colonial Spanish America, with innumerable modern editions in many languages.

11. *Francisco Cervantes de Salazar.* DIÁLOGOS LATINOS. TÚMULO IMPERIAL DE LA GRAN CIUDAD DE MÉXICO. Mexico, 1560.

Cervantes de Salazar (c. 1514 – c. 1575) studied Canon law in Salamanca and taught rhetoric at the University of Osuna, near Seville. He was the first major Humanist who moved to New Spain. In 1553, he became professor of rhetoric in the newly created University of Mexico. A year later he took holy orders, and from 1572 he served as university rector. Because of his intimate knowledge of Mexico, Cervantes de Salazar was commissioned by the Crown to write a *Chronicle of New Spain.* He managed to write six books on the conquest of Mexico, but the work was never completed. It can be considered, however, the first historiographical work in the Humanist tradition and style produced in New Spain. Cervantes de Salazar made extensive use of written sources, especially Gómara, whom he follows in his view of the conquest of Mexico as a double triumph for Spain and the Church, but he obtained additional infor-

FIGURE 8. Bernal Díaz del Castillo. *Historia verdadera de la conquista de la Nueva España*. Madrid, [1632]. The map shown here identifies the New World as "America" instead of the more common name, "The Indies." On the left side, above the image of Cortés, a title says "manu," Latin for "with his hand," giving him credit for the military conquest of Mexico. On the right, Father Bartolomé de Olmedo, a Mercedarian friar who accompanied Cortés's army, is represented with a title reading "ore," Latin for "with his mouth," giving him credit for being the pioneer in the spiritual conquest of the Mexicans.

mation from witnesses like Cortés himself and Indians who knew the ancient rituals. To this he added thoughtful descriptions of the fauna and the flora of Mexico, the result of his own observations.

Although the *Crónica* remained in manuscript form until this century, Cervantes de Salazar published a collection of three Latin dialogues entitled *Diálogos latinos. Túmulo imperial de la gran ciudad de México* (Mexico, 1560) dealing with various aspects of life in the city at that time as well as substantial comments on the ancient Mexicans.

12. *Antonio de Solís.* HISTORIA DE LA CONQUISTA DE MÉXICO. Madrid, 1684.

Solís (1610–1686) possessed a solid Humanistic education received at the University of Salamanca. King Philip II appointed him Secretary of State in 1654. In 1666 he became a priest, and in the last five years of his life he served as official chronicler of the Indies. A historian of the Baroque period, Solís looked upon historical writing as an artistic labor whose goal was an aesthetically perfect product, and he found general histories too diverse in their content to achieve that end. Consequently, he concentrated on the conquest of Mexico, a subject that by the mid-seventeenth century had been almost forgotten. Solís subscribed to Gómara's glorious view of both Cortés and the conquest, but his originality lies in the literary quality of his discourse. His chapters, written in elegant style, are arranged in the manner of a novel, each containing an equal number of events and holding the reader in suspense to the end. The result is what the famous nineteenth-century American historian William Prescott called one of the "most remarkable texts in the Castilian language." For a long time it was used as a textbook for French students of Spanish.

The erudite Chilean bibliographer José Toribio Medina did not hesitate to call Solís's *Historia* "the most popular work ever on the subject of American history." Between 1684 and 1800 more than eighty editions appeared in Spanish, French, Italian, German, Danish, and English. The first English edition, entitled *History of the conquest of Mexico*, was published in London in 1724.

FIGURE 9. Antonio de Solís. *Historia de la conquista de México*. Madrid, 1684. A portrait of King Charles II of Spain is held by two female figures representing Spain on the left (notice the Classical garb and the eagle by her side) and New Spain on the right (notice the Aztec feather headdress and the turkey). The crown topping the portrait of the king rests on two spheres symbolizing his domain in both the Old and the New World.

# III · *About and by the Indians: Ethnography of Mexico*

THE SYSTEMATIC STUDY of foreign cultures by the ethnographers of the ancient world, whose best practioners were the Greek Herodotus and the Roman Polybius, ceased to exist after the fall of the Roman empire. For ten centuries, Europe only managed to produce some accounts by occasional travelers in faraway countries such as Marco Polo's incursion into the Orient and China. The European discovery of America brought about a renewed tradition of interest in foreign peoples, initiated by Columbus himself. Many explorers carefully recorded what they saw in their encounters with the Indians. This body of information, although valuable, was limited by obvious handicaps such as the language problem and the lack of sufficient time to inquire in depth about customs and institutions. A major improvement was to take place after the arrival of twelve Franciscan friars in New Spain in the spring of 1524.

Cortés had asked the emperor to send these twelve apostles with the purpose of beginning a campaign of indoctrination of the Indians into the Christian faith, a spiritual conquest that would complement the recently accomplished military conquest. The twelve set out upon their task immediately with considerable success, and they eventually were able to influence the authorities to protect the Indians against abuses by the white colonists. No less significant was the key contribution of one of them, Fr. Toribio de Motolinía, to historiography. His familiarity with the Indians, with whom the friars lived, soon enabled him to acquire a good grasp of indigenous languages and cultures. In time, other friars followed Motolinía's example and wrote down what they learned, with the result that by the end of the sixteenth century a number of impressive studies had been completed by other Franciscans and Dominicans. To be sure, the purpose of these works was mostly practical. But rather than having political and military value, they were primarily intended to serve as tools for the friars' evangelical mission. The friars correctly thought that their preaching would be greatly helped by a thorough understanding of the Indian way of life and its origins. As such, these works were not meant for public exposure, and most of them remained in manuscript form during the lifetimes of their authors, although they tended to circulate internally within particular religious orders. Today, these ethnographic studies are considered an invaluable contribution to our knowledge of pre-Columbian Mexico. In time, ethnographic studies were also written by laymen, and some of them were published.

As a result of their educational efforts, the friars were also instrumental in the development of a new kind of historiography in Mexico. Several schools for the instruction of the Indians started functioning soon after the conquest. Some of the students acquired a European education, especially those mestizos and Indians of the noble class who attended the prestigious Colegio de Santa Cruz de Tlaltelolco near Mexico City (founded in 1536), whose curriculum included the solid study of Latin. Among the disciplines of Western culture that the students were introduced to was historiography, the techniques of which they applied to the study of their own region or the pre-Hispanic nations. These authors also added a new perspective on the Spanish conquest of Mexico, namely a focus on the plight of the conquered. Their works constitute some of the earliest manifestations of a truly colonial culture, partly Spanish and partly Indian, which forms the dual base of today's Latin America.

FIGURE 10. Antonio de Herrera y Tordesillas. *Historia general de los hechos de las castellanos.* Madrid, 1601–1615. These drawings of the ritual battles between Aztec and Tlaxcaltecan warriors, called "flowered wars," provide accurate details of the soldiers' weapons and uniforms.

13. *Toribio de Motolinía.* HISTORIA DE LOS INDIOS DE NUEVA ESPAÑA. Mexico, 1858.

Motolinía (*c.* 1490–1569) was one of the twelve Franciscans who started the evangelization of New Spain. Throughout his long life he traveled extensively as an indefatigable missionary, and in 1548 he was appointed general vicar of his order in New Spain. He also participated actively in politics. Motolinía learned the Nahuatl language and was the first to collect data on all aspects of Aztec culture. The *Historia*, completed around 1541, was probably a hastily arranged report for the Count of Benavente, a royal counselor, intended as a document to back Franciscan views on the evangelization of the Indians, which frequently clashed with the views of the Dominicans. It is loosely divided into three parts: the first deals with Aztec religious practices, as contrasted with some of their new Christian festivals; the second details the process of conversion into Christianity led by the Franciscans; the third combines a discussion of aspects of the evangelization process with descriptions of the qualities of New Spain and its people.

FIGURE 11. Antonio de Herrera y Tordesillas. *Historia general de los hechos de los castellanos*. Madrid, 1601–1615. The Aztec emperor Montezuma is shown here being carried to Tenochtitlan's main temple.

Motolinía's *Historia* remained unpublished in full until 1858, but manuscript copies were used earlier by the Scottish historian William Robertson (1721–1793) and by Lord Kingsborough, who reproduced 59 pages in Volume IX of his *Antiquities of Mexico* (London, 1830–1848).

14. *Bernardino de Sahagún*. GENERAL HISTORY OF THE THINGS OF NEW SPAIN. London, 1830–1848.

Sahagún (*c.* 1500–1590) went to Mexico in 1529 as a Franciscan missionary, never to return to Spain in his long life. He soon acquired a mastery of the Nahuatl language, which he used to write books of devotion and sermons while teaching Latin at the Colegio de Tlaltelolco. At the age of fifty-seven he began a massive collection of data on Aztec culture by sending a complete questionnaire to hundreds of Indians, interrogating them on all aspects of their culture, a previously unheard of method which anticipated the practices of modern ethnologists. The result of his endeavors was the *Historia general de las cosas de Nueva España*, the most complete ethnological study on Mexico produced in his time, all the more remarkable because in order to be as precise as possible Sahagún wrote it originally in Nahuatl and then translated it with numerous linguistic comments into Spanish. The *Historia* is divided into twelve volumes, covering religious beliefs and rituals as well as social and political institutions. The twelfth book is an account of the conquest of Mexico from the Indian point of view. Unlike other commentators at the time, Sahagún did not interfere with his information by introducing interpretations and value judgments. He delivered instead an uncommonly neutral exposition of facts.

Sahagún's *Historia* remained in manuscript form until the early nineteenth century. It was first published by Carlos María Bustamante in three Spanish volumes (Madrid, 1829–1830), and almost at the same time by Lord Kingsborough in English in Volumes V and VI of his *Antiquities of Mexico*. Today's scholars consider it indispensable for the study of Aztec culture.

15. *Diego Durán*. HISTORIA DE LAS INDIAS DE NUEVA ESPAÑA Y ISLAS DE TIERRA FIRME. Mexico, 1867.

Durán (*c.* 1537–1588) was born in Spain but grew up in New Spain, thus acquiring an intimate knowledge of Indian culture. He entered the Dominican order in 1556 and served as a priest in various towns. Like many friars, he was devoted to protecting the rights of the Indians. A devout and intransigent Christian, Durán wanted a true and complete conversion of the Indians into Christianity without any trace of idolatry, which he suspected was still prevalent in disguised ways. For the purpose of first identifying and then eradicating any manifestation of religious syncretism, he dedicated a lifetime to exhaustive research concerning all aspects of the Aztec religion, using all sorts of Indian sources. Ironically, his unmatched command of his subject resulted in a real understanding of the Indian rites, which he frequently compared with Christian practices, sometimes even describing them in a tone of admiration. Father Durán thought that certain similarities between Aztec and Jewish practices clearly indicated a connection between the two peoples, a belief shared by other friars. He also typically saw the conquest of Mexico as an act of providential design in which God prevailed over the devil.

Nothing is known about what influence, if any, Durán's work had among his contemporaries. Only one manuscript of Durán's *Historia* survived in the National Library in Spain, which the Mexican scholar José Fernando Ramírez published for the first time in 1867.

FIGURE 12. Antonio de Herrera y Tordesillas. *Novus Orbis, sive descriptio Indiae Occidentalis.* Amsterdam, 1622. In contrast to the idealized depictions of native Americans common to European books of this time, Herrera's illustrations are based on drawings by Indian artists. The images shown here, which make up one section of the engraved title page of this book, depict three of the Aztec gods and a pyramid (Enlarged).

FIGURE 13. Juan de Tovar. *Historia de la benida de los yndios.* [Between 1582 and 1587]. The Tovar manuscript illustrates a ritual dance performed by Aztec nobles and priests. The original is in brilliant color.

16. *Juan de Tovar.* HISTORIA DE LA BENIDA DE LOS YNDIOS A POBLAR A MEXICO [MS] [Between 1582 and 1587].

Tovar (*c.* 1546–*c.* 1626) entered the Jesuit order in 1572 and spent his life doing missionary work in Mexico. An expert in the Nahuatl language, he collected pre-Hispanic Aztec codexes and then conducted extensive interrogations with the wise men of Tula, Mexico, and Tezcoco, in order to acquire their full meaning. He also mentions having used the manuscript of a Dominican friar, probably Durán's (see No. 15). The *Historia* begins with the correspondence between the author and José de Acosta, who used Tovar's work in Book VII of his *Historia natural y moral de las Indias* (see No. 44). It consists of four parts. First it contains a history of the Mexicans as told in their oral tradition, ending with the death of

Montezuma and the Noche Triste (June, 1520). This is complemented by an essay on the rites, ceremonies, and gods that existed before the arrival of the Spanish. The third part is a unique collection of fifty-one watercolor paintings that illustrate the text. They seem heavily influenced by Mexican drawing techniques. The final part is dedicated to the study of the Aztec Calendar, and contains several drawings and commentaries.

This manuscript remained unknown to historians until 1840, when the Spanish scholar Pascual de Gayangos saw it in the house of its owner, the British collector Sir Thomas Phillipps. It was acquired by the John Carter Brown Library in 1947.

17. *Diego de Landa*. RELATION DES CHOSES DE YUCATAN. Paris, 1864.

Landa (1524–1579) was one of the first Franciscan missionaries in the Yucatan peninsula, a Maya territory finally conquered in 1545, where he became bishop of Mérida in 1573. Unlike Aztec culture, which was in its full splendor at the time of the arrival of the Europeans, the Mayas had suffered a long period of decline before the sixteenth century, probably due to internal warfare. Landa has been both indicted and praised for his actions toward the Mayas. On the one hand, he ordered many Indian manuscripts destroyed for fear they could be used in pagan rites; on the other, he was a devoted protector of the Indians and a diligent student of Mayan culture, the language of which he knew well. The *Relation* deals with the Spanish discovery and conquest of Yucatan seen from the Indian perspective. It is also a well-informed survey of Maya history, beliefs, and customs, for which he used Indian informants. Of special importance is his study of Maya hieroglyphics and the calendar, which is the basis for all scholarly studies produced since.

The only surviving manuscript from Landa is a 1616 partial copy of a larger original that itself has not survived but that was used by Herrera y Tordesillas (see No. 46) and other historians. The manuscript was found at the Academia de la Historia in Madrid by Abbé Charles-Étienne de Braseur de Bourbourg, who published it for the first time in his own French translation.

18. *Fernando Alvarado Tezozomoc*. STORIA DI MESSICO. Italy, 1842.

Alvarado Tezozomoc (c. 1519 – c. 1599) was a mestizo of double high lineage, the son of Diego de Alvarado, a family of illustrious conquistadors, and Francisca de Motecuzoma, the daughter of emperor Montezuma II. He served most of his life as an interpreter in the royal *audiencia* in Mexico City. Alvarado Tezozomoc wrote historical works in both Nahuatl and Spanish. His *Crónica mexicana*, written in Spanish, deals with the history of the Aztec nation from the end of the fourteenth century until the arrival of Cortés in 1519. As a proud descendant of the Aztec monarchs, the *Crónica* exalts the splendor of Aztec culture and claims a dominant role for Mexico-Tenochtitlan in the Triple Alliance that constituted the so-called Aztec empire. Alvarado Tezozomoc used a variety of written Nahuatl sources, which is reflected in the style of his prose. When he is translating from poems and songs, his work has a poetic tone; when he gets his information from old pictures, his style assumes a more descriptive mode.

The *Crónica mexicana* remained in manuscript form until the nineteenth century, when it was published in Spanish, English, Italian, and French editions. This Italian edition, entitled *Storia di Messico*, appeared in Volume X of Marmochi's *Raccolta di viaggi*.


19. *Fernando de Alva Ixtilxochitl.* HORRIBLES CRUELDADES DE LOS CONQUISTADORES DE MÉXICO Y DE LOS INDIOS QUE LOS AUXILIARON. Mexico, 1829.

Alva Ixtilxochitl (c. 1568–1648), a mestizo from Texcoco, was the grandson of Ixtilxochitl, the last lord of Texcoco, who had sided with Cortés during the siege of Tenochtitlan. After graduating with honors from the Colegio de Santa Cruz de Tlaltelolco, he appealed to the Spanish crown for recompense for the services rendered to it by his ancestor. King Philip III gave him a landgrant, and he was made governor of Texcoco in 1612, and of Tlalmanalco in 1617. Alva Ixtilxochitl's major historical work was originally written in Nahuatl. His *Historia chichimeca*, which traces the history of the Chichimeca nation from its origins to their settling in central Mexico as members of the Triple Alliance, provides useful information obtained from Nahuatl documents and oral records. In the final chapter of his *Historia general de la Nueva España*, he covers the conquest of Mexico from a new perspective that mirrors his mestizo condition: on the one hand he is consistently critical of the injustices of the conquistadors toward the Indians, but at the same time he feels proud of his noble ancestor's role in helping Cortés's army, and he also subscribes to the Spanish view of the conquest as a positive development because it brought along the Christian faith.

Alva Ixtilxochitl did not publish any of his works during his lifetime. The last chapter of his *Historia general* was published in 1829 by Carlos María Bustamante, who gave it the rather strange title *Horrible cruelties of the conquistadors of Mexico and the Indians who helped them*. It is usually known as the Thirteenth Relation. Lord Kingsborough published an English translation in Volume IX of his *Antiquities of Mexico*.


20. *Diego Muñoz Camargo.* HISTORIA DE LA CIUDAD Y REPÚBLICA DE TLAXCALA. Mexico, 1892.

Muñoz Camargo (d. c. 1612) was a mestizo of noble lineage. His father was a Spanish royal officer, and his mother a direct descendant of Maxixcatzin, one of the four lords of the Republic of Tlaxcala. He was a wealthy man and served many years as governor of Tlaxcala.

His *Historia* is divided into two parts. In the first one, dealing with the prehispanic history of Tlaxcala, Muñoz Camargo gathered materials from the oral tradition and wrote on the customs, religious beliefs, and practices, of the Indians, including also a genealogy of the lords of Tlaxcala. The second part starts with the arrival of the Spanish. After some initial opposition to Cortés, the republic of Tlaxcala, which had managed to stay independent against the threat of the Triple Alliance of Mexico, became the most important ally of the conquistadors in their campaign of conquest. Muñoz Camargo's history dwells on this collaboration in order to support his claims to the Crown for the special privileges promised by the Spanish on behalf of that alliance. The *Historia* ends abruptly in the year 1590.

Muñoz Camargo's unfinished manuscript was known to Fr. Juan de Torquemada, who used it extensively in his *Monarquía yndiana* (No. 50). Henri Ternaux-Compans published a deficient French edition in 1860. The edition by Alfredo Chavero presented here is the first with the complete text in Spanish.

21. *Pedro Sánchez de Aguilar.* INFORME CONTRA IDOLORUM CULTORES DEL OBISPADO DE YUCATAN. Madrid, 1639.

Sánchez de Aguilar (1555–1648) belonged to two illustrious families of conquistadors—his grandfather was one of the twelve founders of Mérida. After getting a higher degree in theology at the University of Mexico, Sánchez served as priest in several parishes in Yucatan and as dean of the Mérida cathedral. He later went to Spain as procurator general of Yucatan at the Royal Court, where he presented this *Informe*, written in both Latin and Spanish. Sánchez contends, as did Landa (No. 17), that idolatry was still pervasive among the Maya and was not being repressed sufficiently by the civilian authorities. He was of the opinion that the Spanish generally underestimated the capacity of the Indians to understand properly the Christian religion, and hence they were less vigorous than they should be in taking steps to eradicate paganism. To prove his point he cited the case of his own grammar instructor, Gaspar Antonio de Herrera, an Indian teacher, interpreter, and organist. He also described in admiring tones "the great, famous, and astounding edifices of stone and mortar, and hewn stone, figures and statues of carved stone left in Oxumal (Uxmal) and Chichininiza (Chichen Itza)." Sánchez, who knew the Mayan language well, provides a long list of superstitions he had recorded. Some are rather odd, such as the habit of pulling out some eyelashes and blowing them towards the sun, believing this will retard the setting of the sun; but others are more practical, such as the various remedies used by medicine-men against rattlesnakes bites.

# IV · *The Land of the Inca: The Conquest of Peru*

EUROPEAN KNOWLEDGE of the Andean region was still non-existent in 1522, when Pascual de Andagoya led the first sea expedition from Panama along the Pacific coast of South America. He went only as far south as today's Colombia, an area then called Pirú or Birú, but heard vague reports of rich and populated lands farther to the south. The long and arduous process of exploration and eventual Spanish domination of the territory of the Inca Empire, known as Tahuantinsuyo, was due largely to the determination of Francisco Pizarro, who in the course of seven years led three expeditions to that area. The third expedition, begun in 1531, finally reached the heart of the empire, which at the time was torn by political dissension. Using the strategy Cortés had followed, Pizarro audaciously seized the Inca Atahualpa in Cajamarca, thus depriving the state of its head. The military campaign ended a few months after the capture, when Spanish troops entered Cuzco in November 1533. Pizarro was able to send a rich treasure to Emperor Charles V, and Europeans quickly came to look upon Peru as a paradise with unlimited quantities of precious metals. However, Peru was soon to be the tragic setting for both Indian revolts and internal warfare among the conquistadors for some twenty years. In time, the name Peru acquired a dual association, a land of both splendor and tragedy.

Pizarro, unlike Cortés, was illiterate and thus could not write his own version of the events he experienced. Historical writing about the conquest of Peru began with soldier chroniclers who participated in the conquest. Their main concern was to narrate the events of the conquest, but without exception they also provided geographic data and descriptions of Inca buildings, customs, and institutions. Once the conquest had been accomplished, interest in the immediate events merged with increased attention to the study of ancient Peru itself, a tendency that culminated in Pedro Cieza de León's book on Inca history, the first of its kind. As in the case of Mexico, a third kind of historical writing quickly followed, in which the authors were partly or completely Indian, and thus managed to offer a view of both ancient and contemporary Peru from a perspective other than the Spanish.

22. LIBRO ULTIMO DEL SUMMARIO DELLE INDIE OCCIDENTALI. Venice, 1534.

This account is the first published report on the conquest of Peru. Altough anonymous, it has been attributed to Cristóbal de Mena, a captain in Pizarro's army who arrived in Spain in December 1533 with news of the conquest. The report narrates the events from the preparation for the expedition to the recent imprisonment of the Inca Atahualpa. It is written from a soldier's point of view in a personal tone similar to that of a modern journalist's eyewitness report and manages to capture the tense atmosphere of the conquest. It is particularly rich in details about the military operations culminating in the capture of the Inca leader and the ransom demanded by Pizarro for his liberation, consisting of vast amounts of bullion sent from Cuzco and Pachacamac.

The account was first published in Seville in 1534. In the same year, an Italian translation appeared in Venice, as the third part of a longer work about the New World. It was reprinted in Rome in 1535 and then by G. B. Ramusio in Venice in 1556. In 1545 a French translation with a map of Peru was published under the title *L'histoire de la terre neuve du Peru en l'Inde Occidentale*, and finally, an English abstract was included in the fourth volume of Purchas's *His Pilgrimes* in 1625.

23. *Francisco de Xerez.* VERDADERA RELACION DE LA CONQUISTA DEL PERU Y PROVINCIA DEL CUZCO LLAMADA LA NUEVA CASTILLA. Seville, 1534.

Xerez (b. 1500) went to the New World at an early age and worked as a scribe in Central America. He accompanied Pizarro on his three expeditions, and on the last one served as his personal secretary. Xerez was commissioned to write a detailed account of the conquest, which he completed in 1533. A year later he took it to Spain (along with the Inca treasure that Pizarro sent to the emperor), and it was quickly published in Seville. Xerez's position as secretary is reflected in the style of his narration, which has been characterized as distant and cold, but also precise and objective. As an official account of the conquest to February 1533, Xerez recounted what he witnessed, without taking sides, and he does not mention his own participation in the conquest. The report also includes the first published information on the life and customs of the Peruvian Indians. As usual, this account is fairly objective in things pertaining to civilian life and less with regard to Inca religion.

Xerez's work had a profound and lasting influence on all subsequent histories of Peru, and the *Verdadera relación* is widely regarded as the foundation of all texts dealing with the region and its conquest. An Italian translation appeared in 1535. Although widely known to German, French, and English historians of Peru, the first editions in those languages did not appear until the nineteenth century.

24. *Pedro Sancho.* RELATIONE PER SUA MAESTA. [Venice, 1556].

Nothing is known about Sancho de Hoz (d. 1547?) before he enrolled in Pizarro's third expedition. When Francisco de Xerez was sent to Spain in 1533, Sancho replaced him as Pizarro's secretary, and as such he was commissioned to write a continuation of the official account of the conquest updated to July of 1534. The major development in this period was the march of the Spaniards from Cajamarca to Cuzco. Sancho had already written the official report on the ransom of the Inca Atahualpa, which he incorporated into his account. Sancho de Hoz is

FIGURE 14. Francisco de Xerez. *Verdadera relacion de la conquista del Peru y provincia del Cuzco llamada la Nueva Castilla*. Seville, 1534. This woodcut title page shows the meeting between the Inca, Atahualpa, and the Spanish forces at Cajamarca in Peru.

somewhat less objective than his predecessor, in that he shows a clear partiality towards Pizarro, whose point of view he takes and whose actions he justifies. He portrays the Inca ruler, for instance, as a cruel tyrant over his subjects, which enables him to present the Spanish conquest of Peru as a liberation. Still, his remarkable descriptive abilities emerge in his descriptions of the Peruvian seashore, the province of Callao, and above all his famous description of Cuzco under the Incas at the end of his relation, the first such attempt by a Spanish chronicler to reconstruct Peruvian society before the conquest. Imitating Cortés's praise of Tenochtitlan, Sancho deems Cuzco a most beautiful, large, and monumental city, even by the highest Spanish standards. Its city walls and the fortress on the rocky hill are described not only as impregnable, but without rival in all of Europe in size and in beauty.

The original Spanish text of the *Relatione* was lost, but Giovanni Battista Ramusio incorporated an Italian translation in the third volume of his *Navigationi et viaggi*. From this edition an English translation was published in 1655, and a Spanish one by Joaquín García Icazbalceta in Mexico City in 1848.

25. *Nicolao de Albenino*. VERDADERA RELACION: DE LO SUSSEDIDO EN LOS REYNOS Y PROVINCIAS DEL PERU. Seville, 1549.

Very little is known about Albenino (b. 1514 ?), other than that he was an Italian exile from Florence, where he had been associated with the Medici family. In June of 1548 he wrote a private letter about the most recent developments during the Peruvian civil war. In a direct and clear style, the letter tells of the three major conflicts between the years 1544 and 1548: the arrival in Peru of Viceroy Núñez Vela to pacify the country and his defeat and death at the hands of the rebel Gonzalo Pizarro, Francisco's brother; the war between Pizarro and captain Diego Centeno; and finally, the successful campaign by the new governor, Pedro de la Gasca, who managed to put an end to Gonzalo Pizarro's rebellion. The letter was privately addressed to Fernán Xuárez, a churchman living in Seville, who upon realizing the importance of the news it contained, gave it immediately to the press.

Albenino made no pretense that he was writing history, and in fact his letter was quickly forgotten. And yet, because of the timing of its publication it circulated widely, very much like a modern magazine.

26. *Pedro de Cieza de León*. PARTE PRIMERA DE LA CHRONICA DEL PERU. Seville, 1553.

Undoubtedly, the foremost soldier-chronicler of Peru was Cieza de León (1518–1554), who was born in Extremadura, Spain, and lived in South America from the age of thirteen. As a soldier he accompanied La Gasca in his campaign against Gonzalo Pizarro and took careful

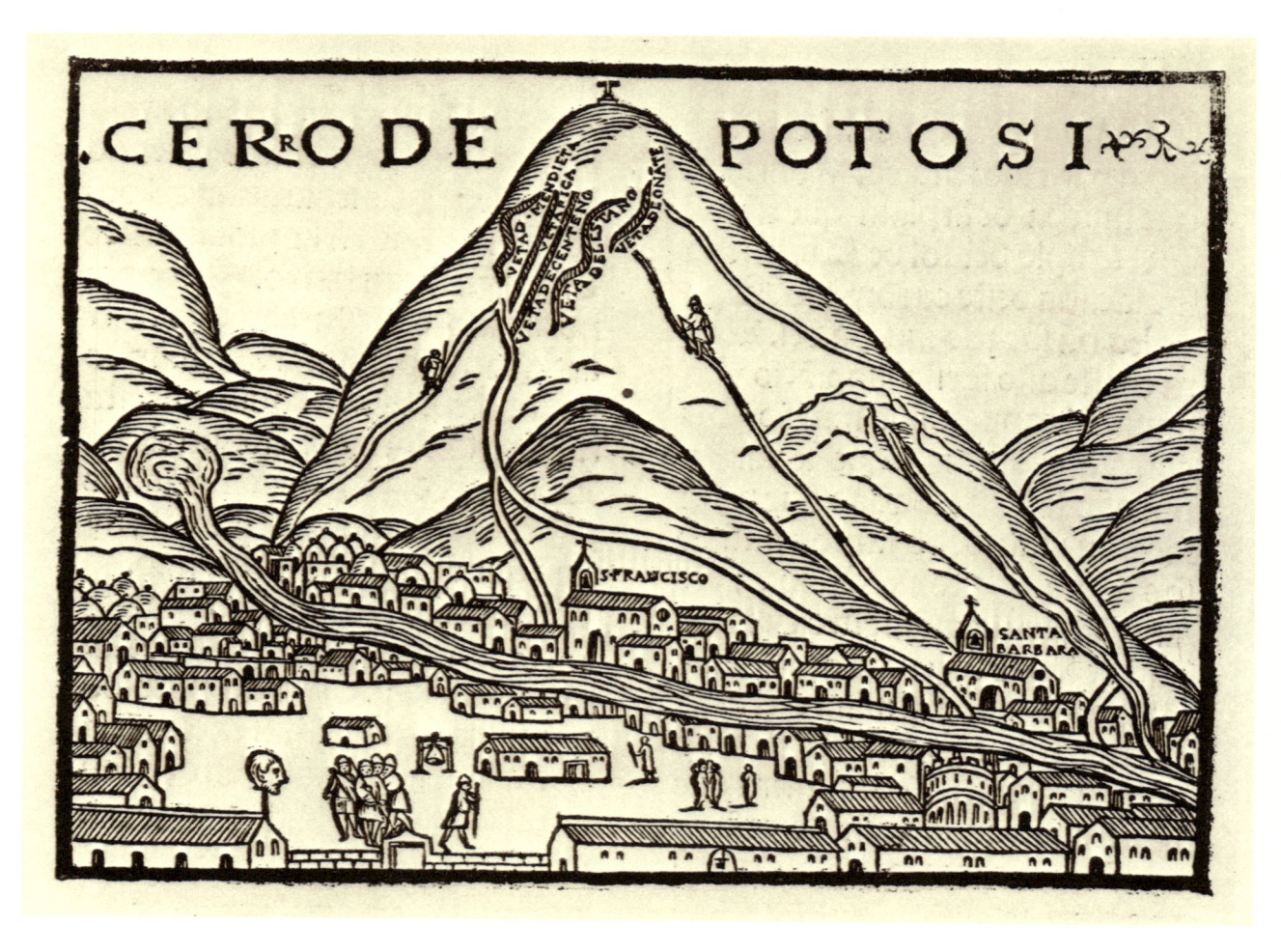

FIGURE 15. Pedro de Cieza de León. *Parte primera de la chronica del Peru.* Seville, 1553. Spaniards discovered extremely rich silver mines at Potosí in 1547. The newly created boom town became instantly famous throughout Europe. Potosí, the author explains, means "mountain" in Quechua, the language of the Indians of Peru. The main silver ores of Potosí hill are drawn and named.

notes on all the events he witnessed. After the end of the civil war, he travelled extensively throughout Peru in order to collect information on both the conquest and the Inca world, with the clear intent of writing the first major history of Peru. When he returned to Spain in 1550, he managed to publish only the first part of his work in Seville, where he lived the rest of his short life. Part I is a thorough description of the land and the people of Peru. It includes both the cities founded by the Spaniards, such as Lima and Quito, and the first documented descriptions of Inca cities and their customs. His wealth of information is the result of personal observation, the scrutiny of reports and official papers, and oral reports from Quechua Indians.

Cieza de León's work was a major success and made him instantly famous. It was reprinted in three separate editions, appearing in Antwerp in 1554, and a year later in an Italian translation published in Rome. The first English edition, entitled *The seventeen years travels of Peter de Cieza*, appeared in 1709. Parts II, III, and IV of the *Chronica* deal respectively with Inca civilization, the Spanish discovery and conquest of Peru, and the civil wars between the Spaniards. They survived in manuscript form and were known to early historians, but they have been published only in the last two centuries.

27. *Agustín de Zárate.* HISTORIA DEL DESCUBRIMIENTO Y CONQUISTA DEL PERU. Antwerp, 1555.

Agustín de Zárate (b. 1514) was a high official who served as Secretary to the Royal Council of Castile for fifteen years. In 1543 Charles V sent him to Peru along with Blasco Núñez Vela, the first viceroy of Peru, to oversee finances. Although a prudent man, he could not avoid getting involved in the ongoing conflict, and he apparently favored Gonzalo Pizarro's faction. In 1545 he returned to Spain, bringing with him a considerable collection of personal notes and other documents about the civil war. With the help of these and other published sources, Zárate composed a history in seven chapters, starting with the Spanish discovery of Peru and ending with the death of Gonzalo Pizarro and the restoration of royal authority by Governor Pedro de la Gasca. Zárate, who wrote in an elegant and clear style, painfully avoided making judgments on the events he described. Aware of the dangers involved in writing about such recent and controversial matters, he expressed a reluctance to publish his history during his lifetime, but a manuscript copy of it was read by Prince Philip, the future King Philip II of Spain, who liked it so much that he ordered its publication.

Zárate's *Historia* was well received, and in 1577 it was reprinted in Seville. An Italian translation published in Venice in 1563, and an English translation published by T. Nicholas in London in 1581, are proof of its quick popularity outside of Spain.

28. *Diego Fernández.* PRIMERA, Y SEGUNDA PARTE, DE LA HISTORIA DEL PERU. Seville, 1571.

Fernández (*c.* 1520 – *c.* 1581), also known as "el Palentino," went to Perú in 1553 to work as the city scribe. He soon was drawn into the last stages of the civil war, in which he took active part as a soldier defending the side of the king against the insurrection of Francisco Hernández Girón (1553–1554). Once the long conflict had come to an end, Fernández was commissioned in Peru to write a history of the most recent events. This he completed in Spain, under the sponsorship of Francisco Tello de Sandoval, president of the Council of the Indies, who provided him with access to official documents. Also included in the *Historia* as an appendix to the second volume is the first published genealogy of Inca rulers. In his introduction, Fernández described the difficulty of writing about conflicts in which the protagonists still bear deeply felt animosities and would not appreciate his efforts to remain objective.

# PRIMERA, Y SEGVNDA PARTE, DE LA HISTORIA

DEL PERV, QVE SE MANDO ESCREuir, à Diego Fernandez, vezino dela ciudad de Palencia. Cōtiene la primera, lo succedido en la Nueua España y enel Perù, sobre la execucion de las nucuas leyes: y el allanamiento, y castigo, que hizo el Presidente Gasca, de Gonçalo Piçarro y sus sequaces.
LA SEGVNDA, CONTIENE, LA TYRANNIA Y ALçamiento delos Contreras, y don Sebastiā de Castilla, y de Francisco Hernādez Giron: con otros muchos acaescimientos y successos. Dirigido à la. C. R. M. del Rey DON PHILIPPE nuestro Señor.

Con Preuilegio Real de Castilla, y Aragon, y delas Indias.

Fue impresso en Seuilla en Casa de Hernando diaz en la calle de la Sicrpe. Año de 1 5 7 1.

FIGURE 16. Diego Fernández. *Primera, y segunda parte, de la historia del Peru.* Seville, 1571. The coat of arms of the Spanish monarchs was often used to decorate the title pages of history books.

Unfortunately, his fears proved well-founded: Pizarro's supporters accused his well-documented history of presenting an unfavorable view of some of their members. Legal action was taken, and as a result the *Historia* was banned immediately after publication.

Most copies of the work were seized and destroyed, and hence the book did not become known to the general public even though a few historians in Fernández's time used it extensively. Several Spanish editions have appeared in this century, but the *Historia* remains largely unknown outside of non-Hispanic countries.

29. *Miguel Cabello de Balboa.* HISTOIRE DU PEROU. Paris, 1840.

Cabello de Balboa (c. 1535–1605) was a veteran of the European wars before he went to the New World in 1566. He later became a priest, and in 1578 he settled in Quito, where he must have begun his study of Inca history. In 1586 he completed his work entitled *Miscelánea antártica y origen de los indios y de los Incas del Perú*, divided into three parts. The first two are highly rhetorical discussions of the creation of the world and the origins of the American Indians in the second of which he ventured the hypothesis that Asians had migrated into the New World. The third part is a history of Peru before the Spanish conquest. Cabello de Balboa's sources included a copy of Cristóbal de Molina's unpublished manuscript entitled *Fábulas y ritos de los Incas* as well as other oral material he had collected. His work lacks organization and a critical scrutiny of his sources, but it is highly valuable as one of the earliest attempts to collect information on Quechua Indian traditions and legends.

The *Miscelánea* remained in manuscript form until the nineteenth century, when the French historian Henri Ternaux-Compans published his translation into French of the third part with the title *Histoire du Perou*.

30. *Garcilaso de la Vega.* COMMENTARIOS REALES . . . DE LOS YNCAS. Lisbon, 1609.

A mestizo of double nobility, Garcilaso (1539–1616), also known as "the Inca," was the son of a Spanish captain from a distinguished family and an Inca princess. He grew up in Cuzco, where he acquired a Renaissance education in Latin and Spanish as well as direct exposure to Quechua language and culture. In 1560 he left Peru never to return. For many years he served as a captain in Philip II's army in Italy, but later he settled in Córdoba, where he dedicated his life to study and writing and became a renowned Humanist. The *Commentarios* was the first major history of pre-Columbian Peru actually to be published. Using both written and oral sources as well as the recollections of his own youth, he provided thorough accounts of the Inca past, as well as extensive studies on religion, politics, economics, and all levels of social life. Garcilaso was aware that his work superseded that of former historians of Peru, whom he accuses of not having sufficient knowledge of the Inca civilization. His cul-

FIGURE 17. Garcilaso de la Vega. *Le commentaire royal, ou l'histoire des Yncas.* Paris, 1633. In the scene above the depiction of the great Inca, Manco Capac, and his wife, there is a religious procession and (top left) a group of Peruvian Indians worshipping the Sun god.

tural syncretism emerges in his vision of Inca culture as a sustained heroic expansion similar to that of the Roman Empire—he explicitly refers to Cuzco as the other Rome—whose goal was to civilize the territory around it. Inca expansion is thus perceived as a process that culminated in the providential arrival of Europeans and Christianity. Garcilaso's brilliant prose reflects his profound knowledge of Classical and Renaissance historiography.

The success of the *Commentarios* quicky established its author as a major historian in Europe. Two French editions were published in Paris in 1633 and 1658, and the first English edition appeared in London in 1688. A second volume of the *Commentarios,* entitled *Historia general del Perú*, dealt with the Spanish conquest and the civil wars. It was completed close to his death, and was published posthumously in Córdoba in 1617.

31. *Felipe Guamán Poma de Ayala.* NUEVA CORONICA Y BUEN GOBIERNO. Paris, 1936.

Poma de Ayala (*c.* 1530–*c.* 1615) was a Peruvian Indian of humble origin, although he claimed direct descent from royal Inca lineage. Little is known about his life, but he seems to have worked mostly as an interpreter. He apparently accepted the Christian faith genuinely, yet he frequently criticized the Church and was resentful towards Spaniards and mestizos. In contrast to Spanish or half-Spanish authors, he espoused a decidedly negative view of the conquest, an attitude that has been appropriately termed "resistance writing." Poma de Ayala's work is divided into two parts. The *Nueva corónica* is a history of pre-Columbian Peru, including the era prior to the Incas, and it ends with a full description of ancient rituals. The second part, entitled *Buen gobierno,* is an indictment of the Spanish invaders, with a complete account of the abuses suffered by the Indians. Poma de Ayala's prose is defective, but he more than compensates for his linguistic limitations in Spanish with hundreds of highly expressive illustrations that explain his text. Since most graphic material from ancient Peru has been lost, Poma de Ayala's drawings are a legacy of the utmost importance for the study of Peruvian ethnography, and the discovery of this work in the twentieth century was an event of the first magnitude.

Poma de Ayala's history was completely unknown to historians until the only surviving manuscript was found in the Royal Library of Copenhagen, Denmark, in 1908. A facsimile edition published in Paris in 1936 made his drawings known for the first time.

# V · *The Continental Empire*

THE IMPERIAL EXPANSION of Spain in the New World occurred at a pace rarely matched in world history. One hundred years after Columbus's first crossing of the ocean, Spain, a small European country of no more than eight million people, had managed to explore, conquer, and colonize a distant and vast territory more than ten times her size and with a far greater population. What Columbus thought to be some Asian islands in 1492 had soon become two new continents vastly larger than Europe itself. By the end of the sixteenth century, Spain dominated much of that land, from California to Chile and from Florida to Patagonia. The *Indias Occidentales*, the Western Indies, thus became the first maritime empire, one where the metropolis managed to impose its language and culture over nations and people three thousand miles away across an ocean that rather than a barrier had quickly become a maritime highway. With the success of Spanish expansion, a completely new period, one characterized by European domination, changed forever the destiny of the American continents.

The quick pace of expansion was made possible by Spain's ability to establish settlements under its rule immediately following a region's conquest. These settlements, established both in former Amerindian cities, such as Mexico City or Cuzco, and in new ones, such as Panama or Lima, instantly became bases for further land and sea expeditions. While crown officers, churchmen, and some settlers quickly moved in to solidify colonial rule in the new outposts, a small but indefatigable group of some twenty thousand ubiquitous conquistadors continued to spread the Spanish presence in the New World with a restless activity that took them from one campaign to the next without stop. The first base of all, the Caribbean islands, were the launching site for expeditions to Florida and the Atlantic Coast of North America, Mexico and the Yucatan, Central America, and Venezuela. New Spain, whose conquest had been initiated from Cuba, became the base for further exploration of the North American South, northern Central America, and Pacific expeditions to the California coast and Asia. Castilla del Oro (Panama) expanded throughout Central America, and then made possible the conquest of both Peru and New Granada (Colombia). Peru then became the base for the exploration of the Amazon region and the conquest of Chile, Paraguay, and the Río de la Plata region.

A vast number of reports, letters, accounts, and histories serve as testimony of the successes and tribulations of the New World explorers, and their encounters—many times violent—with the native inhabitants. Understandably, most of the early works were written by protagonists of expeditions and military campaigns whose primary interest was making the facts known, justifying their own role in the events, and ultimately getting due recognition for their services to the crown. After the exploration, conquest, and eventual settlement by the Spanish, a good number of authors tended to shift their interest towards the collection of natural, ethnic, and linguistic information about the territories.

32. *Alvar Núñez Cabeza de Vaca.* RELACION. Zamora, 1542.

Núñez Cabeza de Vaca (16th cent.) was the treasurer of the first major expedition organized to explore the coast between Florida and Mexico, lead by Pánfilo de Narváez. The explorers landed near Tampa Bay on April 14, 1528, and from there hiked to an area near present-day Tallahassee, but swamps and hostile Indians forced them to return to the coast and sail west in improvised boats. After most of the remaining men, including Narváez, died on the Texas coast, Núñez was captured by Indians. This capture marked the beginning of an extraordinary adventure of endurance, skill, and cultural adaptation, in which Núñez and four other survivors worked their way up among the Indians from being virtual slaves to the noble status of healers. The fivesome then began a long march to the west through unknown territory. Using Indian means of survival and orientation, they crossed Texas, the desert of Sonora, and the Sierra Madre, finally reaching a Spanish outpost on the Pacific coast eight years after the beginning of the expedition. Due to the highly unusual facts it described, Núñez's accurate tale of hardship and survival, although conveyed in a direct and simple style devoid of mythical allusions, was wrongly believed by some to be fanciful.

Alvar Núñez's 1542 Zamora edition is now one of the rarest books of Spanish colonial history. The relation is commonly known as *Naufragios* ("Shipwrecks"). In 1555 a second edition appeared in Valladolid with the title *Relacion y comentarios*, in which Núñez added an account of his later activity in South America.

33. *Garcilaso de la Vega.* LA FLORIDA DEL YNCA. HISTORIA DEL ADELANTADO HERNANDO DE SOTO. Lisbon, 1605.

Hernando de Soto (1492–1542) was one of the most distinguished captains under Francisco Pizarro in the conquest of Peru. Back in Spain he learned of Núñez Cabeza de Vaca's failed expedition to Florida, and quickly organized another one. Sailing from Havana, Soto and his men landed at Tampa on May 15, 1539, and then proceeded inland until reaching Appalachia. After descending to the Alabama coast, they penetrated into the interior to the northwest, and on May 8, 1541, they were the first Europeans to view the Mississippi River near today's Memphis. Traveling west they reached Arkansas where the cruel winter stopped them, and Soto died of fever. The rest of the expedition returned to the Mississippi and sailed along its course, the remaining survivors finally reaching Tampico, Mexico, in September 1543. After four years of hostilities with the Indians, and unending marches, the expedition had failed to discover the sought-after Fountain of Youth nor any significant riches, but it rendered a most valuable geographic contribution. Garcilaso de la Vega (No. 30) exalts Soto as a Renaissance hero of endurance and courage. Although based on an eye-witness account, Garcilaso's history is at times fanciful and prone to associations with Classical mythology. The work is written in his characteristically learned and elegant style.

34. *Diego López de Cogolludo.* HISTORIA DE YUCATHAN. Madrid, 1688.

López (*c.* 1612–1665) was a Franciscan missionary. He went to the New World in 1634 and spent the rest of his life in Yucatán, where he learned the Mayan language, preaching and teaching philosophy and theology at Mérida. The first three chapters of the *Historia* deal with civil history. The Yucatán peninsula, whose people, the Mayas, remained free of Aztec domination, was conquered by the Spanish in three long campaigns, the first started by Francisco de Montejo in 1527 and the last concluded by his son of the same name in 1545. López used both his access to official papers and previous histories to narrate this part. Chapter four contains a thorough description of the land, the customs, and the beliefs of the Mayan people, whom López thinks descended from the Phoenicians and the Carthaginians. The remaining six chapters are dedicated to the history of the Franciscan order's progress in converting and instructing the Indians, and are written in the laudatory tone typical of religious history (see Chapter VII, below).

35. *Lucas Fernández de Piedrahita.* HISTORIA GENERAL DE LAS CONQUISTAS DEL NUEVO REYNO DE GRANADA. Antwerp, [1688].

Fernández de Piedrahita (1624–1688), a mestizo, was born in Santa Fe (Colombia) and had a distinguished career as a churchman in the New World, serving as bishop of Santa Marta (Colombia) and Panama. For his history he used his direct knowledge of the area as well as many documents, particularly the long and detailed account of the conquest of the territory written by its main conquistador, Gonzalo Jiménez de Quesada, which in the seventeenth century was still in manuscript. The *Historia*, which carries the story forward to 1566, is divided into twelve books. The first two deal with Indian history and are indispensable for the ethnographic understanding of the area. The remaining ten books narrate the events of the conquest: the foundation of Santa Marta by Rodrigo de Bastidas in 1525; Jiménez de Quesada's three-year campaign into the interior, which culminated in the founding of Santa Fe (1539); the creation of the *audiencia* in 1549 and the expansion of Spanish settlements in the region.

FIGURE 18. Diego López de Cogolludo. *Historia de Yucathan.* Madrid, 1688.

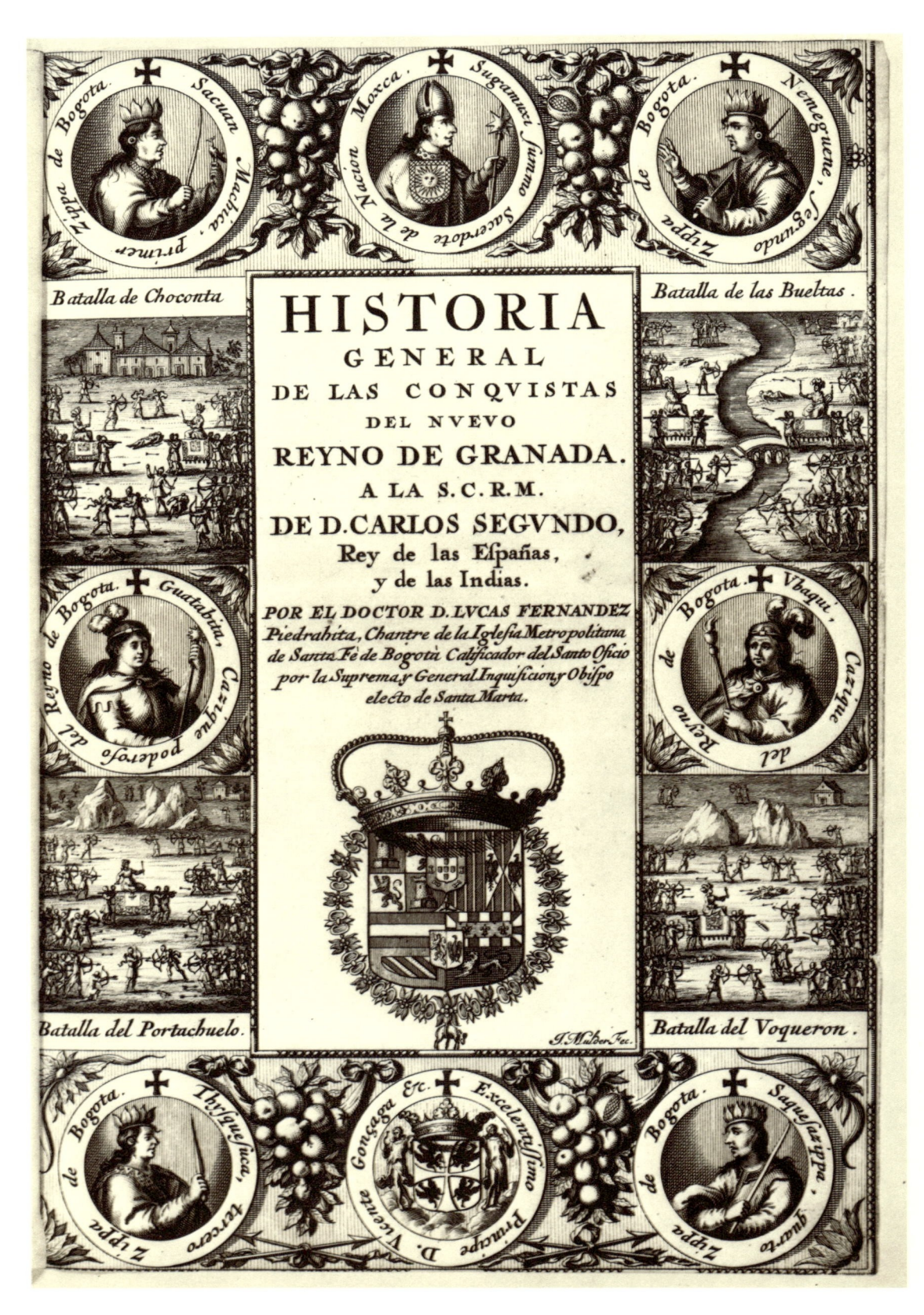

FIGURE 19. Lucas Fernández de Piedrahita. *Historia general de las conquistas del nuevo reyno de Granada*. Antwerp, [1688]. This title page presents portraits of pre-Hispanic rulers, a high priest (top center), and scenes from the four wars of the Spanish conquest.

36. *Manuel Rodríguez*. EL MARAÑON, Y AMAZONAS. Madrid, 1684.

Rodríguez (1633–1701), a Jesuit with long experience in the Amazon area, wrote a history of all the expeditions along the river, from the early ones through those in his own lifetime, using several first-hand accounts. The first expedition was the celebrated trek of Francisco de Orellana, who discovered the sources of the Amazon river in Peru and sailed its complete course with his men in improvised boats in 1542. Because the explorers encountered some women among the Indians who attacked them, the river, also known as Marañón, took the name of the mythical female fighters, the amazons. Another old legend, the one concerning the elusive man of Eldorado, motivated a second expedition twenty years later commanded by Pedro de Ursúa and marred by the rebellion of Lope de Aguirre, who killed Ursúa and ruined the expedition before being executed himself in 1561. Rodríguez's history concentrates on the ensuing expeditions in which his religious order had a prominent role, including Acuña's (No. 37), with the intention of claiming major successes in the evangelization of the Indians.

37. *Cristóbal de Acuña*. NUEVO DESCUBRIMIENTO DEL GRAN RÍO DE LAS AMAZONAS. Madrid, 1641.

Acuña (b. 1597) was born in Burgos, Spain. He entered the Jesuit order at the age of fifteen, and in about 1636 went to the New World. After the kingdoms of Spain and Portugal had been unified under the Spanish monarch in 1580, a project was developed to explore the possibilities of establishing commercial shipping up and down the Amazon, which it was hoped would prove to be a better route than the long and dangerous voyage around the Magellan Straits. Acuña, who was then the rector of the Jesuit college in Quito, joined Pedro Texeira's scientific expedition, which accomplished a remarkable nine-month voyage upstream along the river from Pará to San Francisco del Quito in 1539. Acuña provided descriptions about the fauna and flora, sometimes accurate, such as the *peraque* or electric fish, "which causes the human body to tremble when touching them," and occasionally fanciful, like the *pejebuey* or cowfish, which purportedly feeds its offspring with two breasts and eats grass. But Acuña was at his best as an ethnographer. His tone is at times exalted, as when he envisioned the magnificent river "holding more than one hundred and fifty nations" of different languages as a vast new empire with four kinds of riches: wood, cocoa, tobacco, and sugar. Generally, however, his brief account is rich in information on the Indians, especially their religious rites and their legends.

Soon after the publication of the *Nuevo descubrimiento*, Spain and Portugal again separated. The book was then banished and most printed copies seized (it has become indeed

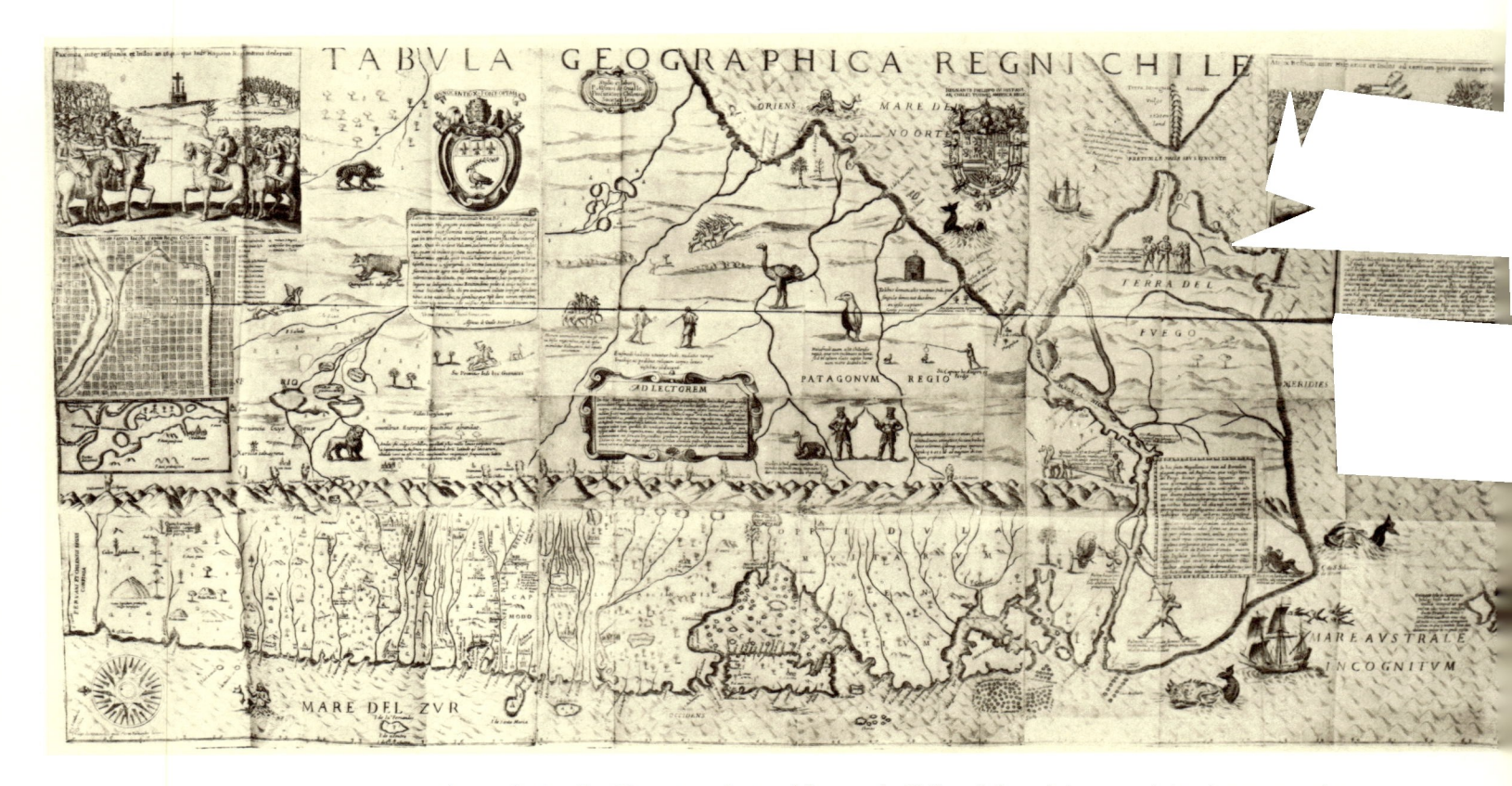

FIGURE 20. Alonso de Ovalle. *Historica relacion del reyno de Chile y de las missiones y ministerios que exercita en el la Compañia de Jesus.* Rome, 1646. This map of Chile, almost four feet long, is oriented with north to the left. Drawings and extensive Latin commentary by Ovalle explain Indian ethnography and the history of the conquest.

one of the rarest), so as to prevent the Portuguese from using Acuña's valuable and precise information. The effort failed, for the book was soon translated and published in several languages.

38. *Alonso de Ovalle.* HISTORICA RELACION DEL REYNO DE CHILE. Rome, 1646.

Ovalle (1601–1651) was born in Santiago, Chile, and joined the Jesuit Order in 1618. He taught philosophy and theology at the San Francisco Javier Seminary in Santiago, where he also served as rector. During a stay in Rome he wrote this book, which was both the first and the best history of Chile written in his time. In the first two chapters he eloquently described the land and the life of its two groups of inhabitants, the Mapuche Indians and the descendants of the Spanish colonists like himself. A history of the conquest follows, from the early expedition of Diego de Almagro (1535–1537), who marched from Cuzco as far south as today's Valparaiso but did not stay to settle, to the long campaign of conquest and settlement directed by Pedro de Valdivia, who also set forth from Peru and founded Santiago in 1541.

FIGURE 21. Alonso de Ovalle. *Historica relacion del reyno de Chile y de las missiones y ministerios que exercita en el la Compañia de Jesus.* Rome, 1646. Chilean Indians playing the ball game known as "chueca."

The last part of the book deals with the missionary work of the Jesuit Order in Chile. The *Histórica relación*, written in an elegant style, has been considered the first expression of a national Chilean identity. It was also one of the most lavishly produced histories of that time; it contains 18 woodcuts, 14 engraved plates, 21 engraved portraits, and a folded map of Chile.

Two editions of Ovalle's history were published simultaneously, one in Spanish and one in Italian, and the book became an instant success that brought him considerable fame. The first English edition, entitled *An historical relation of the kingdom of Chile*, was published by Awnsham Churchill in London in 1703.

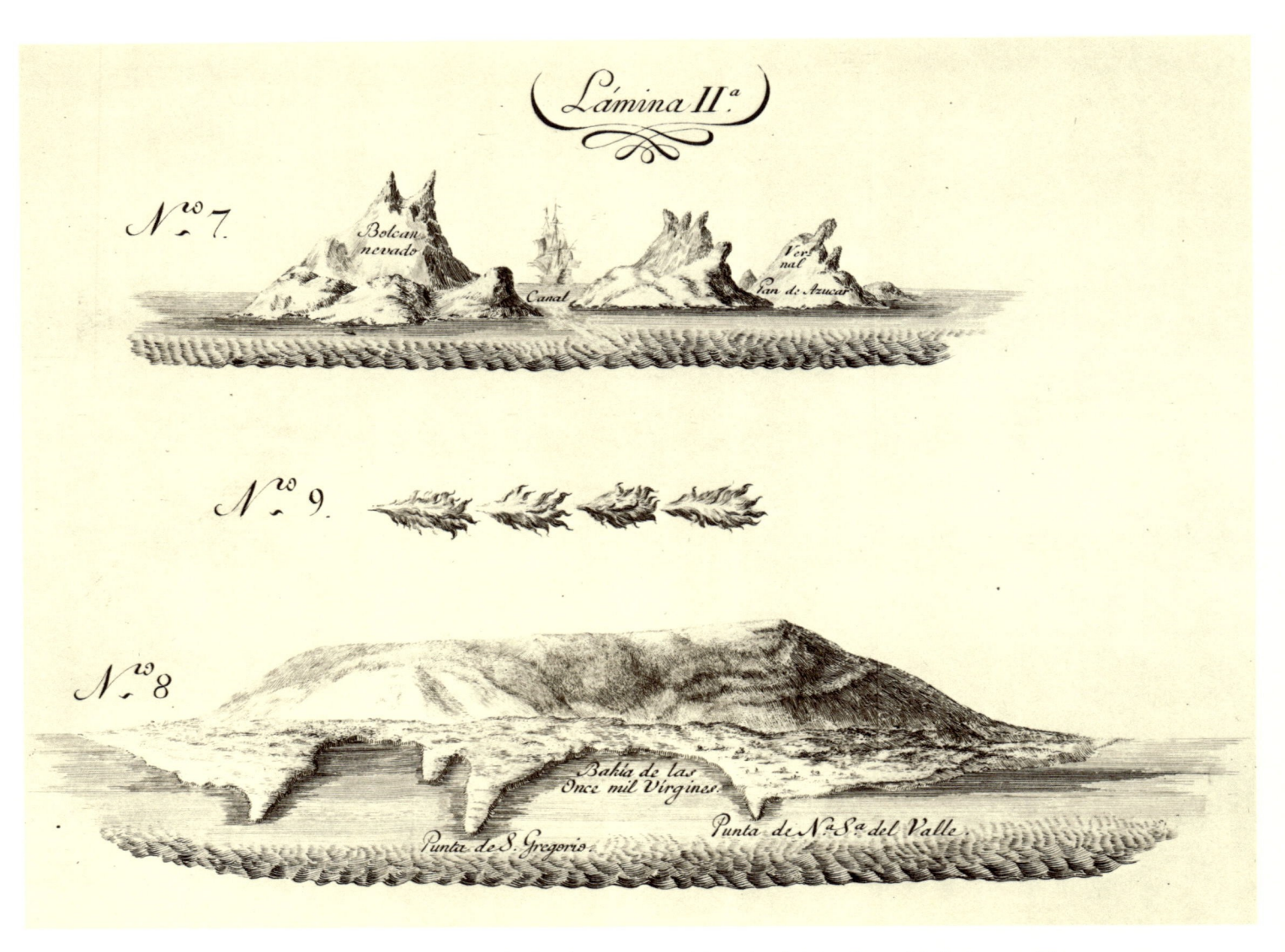

FIGURE 22. Pedro Sarmiento de Gamboa. *Viage al Estrecho de Magallanes.* Madrid, 1768. These engravings focus on the coast of southern Chile.

39. *Pedro Sarmiento de Gamboa.* VIAGE AL ESTRECHO DE MAGALLANES. Madrid, 1768.

Sarmiento de Gamboa (1532?–1608?) was a multitalented man, as proven by his success as a soldier, astrologer, cosmographer, and historian. After Sir Francis Drake had raided the Spanish settlements in the South Pacific in 1579, an important Spanish expedition was launched from Peru both in order to explore the southern Chilean coast and to look for possible sites of settlement that would prevent English attacks. The expedition was to navigate a passage through the Magellan Straits from the Pacific to the Atlantic. Sarmiento served as official cosmographer of the expedition and wrote this splendid report of his navigation, which ended in Spain in August of 1580. It provides detailed descriptions of such maritime concerns as the coastline and sea currents, and can thus be used as a practical guide. Sarmiento anticipated that foreign pirates would enter the Pacific from the straits and threaten Spanish settlements, and he argued for the founding of defensive colonies in the Austral region of Chile, which the conquistadors had not yet reached. After reading the *Viage*, King Philip II authorized Sarmiento to carry out his plans. He founded two towns, Nombre de Jesús and Real Felipe, but the extremely harsh environment and the towns' remoteness prevented them from succeeding.

The *Viage* remained in manuscript until 1768, when Bernardo de Iriarte published it in Madrid. It was used extensively in the eighteenth century by all Spanish expeditions into the area. C. Markham published an English edition for the Hakluyt Society with the title *Narratives of voyages of Pedro Sarmiento de Gamboa to the Straits of Magellan* (London, 1895).

40. *Antonio de Morga.* SUCESOS DE LAS ISLAS FILIPINAS. Mexico, 1609.

In his Bull of 1493, Pope Alexander VI had established a line of demarcation between Spain's and Portugal's rights of possession. Following the Magellan expedition (1519–1522), a hot debate ensued between the two countries about the limits of that line in the Far East, until it was finally agreed that it would run between the Molucca Islands (part of today's Indonesia) and the Philippines. Antonio de Morga (1559–1636), a career royal official, arrived in Manila to serve as the first lieutenant governor of the Philippines, a post he held for eight years. A learned man with a degree in Canon Law from Salamanca, Morga carefully gathered detailed information on the Spanish discovery, conquest, and settlement of the Philippines, which he elaborated in the eight books of his *Historia*. His account, written in an exemplary clear and concise style, covers events starting with the 1564 expedition led by Miguel López de Legazpi and the Augustinian Andrés de Urdaneta, which successfully conquered the islands and named them after Philip II of Spain, to the year 1606. Book VIII is a priceless resource for the history of the islands, natural and ethnographic, in which the author makes a notable attempt to differentiate the multiple ethnic groups and their languages. Morga praises some habits of the Indians, such as their constant bathing, and abhors others, such as their sexual promiscuity. He also records some interesting consequences of the encounter, such as the Pintado Indians' newly acquired habit of wearing shoes and punishing adulterous wives.

# VI · *The Overall View: The Quest for a General History*

THE CHRISTIAN NOTION of universal history, based on the solid unity of the sacred and the profane, had enjoyed much favor throughout the Middle Ages. During the Renaissance, however, many factors contributed to its ultimate decline, namely the Humanist preference for Classical models, the growing nationalist tendencies of the time, and the great geographical discoveries that destroyed the old paradigms. As a result, historical writing in Europe tended to shift its focus from sacred models to national, regional, and local themes. But in the case of Spain, the discovery of the New World made that easy reduction impossible. The Magellan expedition (1519–1522) had irrefutably proven that what Columbus saw was not part of Asia but a new geographical entity of immense proportions. It was inevitable, after some chronicles had dealt with specific themes concerning the New World, that historians would attempt to take a comprehensive view of the new reality then known as the Indies and ultimately to establish its proper place in the history of the world.

Such an enterprise was no easy task, given the enormous variety of both the physical and the human elements of the new continents. Some scholarly historians had the dedication and the discipline to amass an impressive amount of data from documents, histories, and their own experience, but it proved much harder to give all that information a unity. In the case of natural history, the accumulation of data was not structured in the modern systematic way, which was not established until the eighteenth century. And yet, many accurate descriptions of the new flora and fauna were provided, culminating in the *magnum opus* by Nicolás de Monardes that significantly enlarged European knowledge of American nature. In the case of the history of New World peoples, the diversity and isolation of the native inhabitants prevented consideration of them as a single group, so accounts were necessarily organized by convenient principles such as geographic location or the chronology of the native group's conquest by Spain.

The ultimate goal of general histories was to integrate the people of the Old and the New Worlds into a single vision of world history. The early assessment of Peter Martyr, who believed the Indians were the isolated inhabitants of the Classical Golden Age, was quickly dismissed as higher civilizations were found. Fernández de Oviedo, who provided the first description of the distinct natural phenomena of the New World, as well as a condensed narrative of its peoples and the Spanish involvement with them, proposed an integration of the Indies into world history through the mission of converting the Indians to Christianity and their submission to a Spanish monarchy soon to become a universal power, a concept first developed by Hernán Cortés. Others, such as López de Gómara, subscribed to this thesis, while Bartolomé de las Casas, who disapproved of any imperial plans, stressed the universality of human behavior by comparing Amerindian life and institutions with those of the Old

World. The problem of the origin of the native Americans was not quite resolved, however, until José de Acosta advanced a new thesis: the Indians had migrated across the Straits of Anian (Bering) from Asia to America, where they had evolved in isolation from the Old World. Thus the Biblical explanation of the single origin of mankind in the Middle East was preserved.

41. *Gonzalo Fernández de Oviedo y Valdés.* LA HISTORIA GENERAL DE LAS INDIAS. Seville, 1535.

After the success of his *Sumario* (No. 6), Fernández de Oviedo was appointed official chronicler of the Indies in 1532, and he used this position to acquire every kind of information concerning the New World. To this material he added a rich personal experience gained in his numerous travels. The result was the *Historia general*, which can be considered the first general history of the New World. It consisted ultimately of a total of fifty books, of which the 1535 edition included only the first nineteen, dedicated to the history of Columbus's voyages and the Caribbean islands. The twentieth book was published in 1557, and the balance in the nineteenth century. Oviedo was a gifted writer who could gracefully arrange the vast array of information he collected from numerous sources and present it in a clear style. He did not hide his prejudices and his critical opinions of people and political events—all his life he was engaged in a political dispute with Bartolomé de las Casas (No. 43)—although as an ethnographer he was able to remain reasonably objective. Of special importance is the information he provided on the fauna and the flora in America, in which he dismissed many established myths and drew only from his careful observations. He provided the first scientific descriptions of rubber trees, the tobacco plant, and a large number of medicinal extracts and edible plants.

Oviedo's *Historia* became a huge success in Europe. The first English translation of the *Historia*, by Richard Eden, appeared in London in 1555 under the title *General history of the West Indies*. Oviedo became one of the most often quoted and famous of all historians of the New World—Von Humboldt even considered him and Acosta (No. 44) the founders of physical geography.

42. *Francisco López de Gómara.* LA ISTORIA DE LAS INDIAS. Y CONQUISTA DE MEXICO. Saragossa, 1552.

It was López de Gómara (No. 9) who first stated, in the foreword of this book, that the discovery of the New World was the single most important event in world history, with the exception only of the birth of Christ. He praised Spain for its distinguished role in an expansion of the Christian faith unprecedented in world history, a concept of the conquest that

FIGURE 23. Francisco López de Gómara. *La istoria de las Indias.* Saragossa, 1552. The first printed image of a buffalo (Enlarged).

was widely accepted by his European contemporaries. Gómara organized his material geographically, from the Labrador Peninsula to the Magellan Straits, and from the Pacific coast to the Atlantic—a movement that imitated the sign of the cross. In brief and densely written short chapters with individual titles, he condensed a wealth of information on nature and its products, the Amerindians and their customs and language, and the conquest of each territory by the Spaniards. His sources were mostly written accounts—Peter Martyr and, above all, Fernández de Oviedo—but he probably also used the oral accounts of some witnesses in the New World. The *Istoria* contains some illustrations, among them an important world map and the first rendering of a "humped cow," i.e., the American buffalo.

Gómara's book quickly became a classic of its genre, even though the first edition in Spanish was banned by the authorities probably for the continuous praise of Cortés, whose son had become a rebel. In 1556 it was first printed in Italian, and in 1568 in French (Michel de Montaigne used it extensively). In England, however, only the second part of the book, dealing with the conquest of Mexico, was printed in the sixteenth century.

FIGURE 24. Bartolomé de las Casas. *Den Spieghel der Spaense tyrannye, geschiet in West-Indien.* Amsterdam, 1638. This horrifying illustration of the mistreatment of Indians by Spanish colonists in America appeared in a Dutch translation of the *Brevissima relacion*, which also contained a denunciation of Spanish cruelties in the Netherlands (Enlarged).

43. *Bartolomé de las Casas.* BREVISSIMA RELACION DE LA DESTRUYCION DE LAS INDIAS. Seville, 1552.

The son of a nobleman, Las Casas (1474–1556) went to the New World in 1502 in search of wealth. Ten years later his conviction that the Indians were being systematically mistreated led him to become a Dominican friar and to dedicate his long life to the single purpose of protecting the Indians. This he did successfully, both as an influential counselor at the royal court and as an author of numerous essays that earned him the title of "Apostle of the Indians." Las Casas abhorred not only the exploitation of the Indians by the Spanish but eventually came to question the conquest in general, favoring instead a peaceful Christian crusade in which he believed the Indians would convert freely. The *Brevissima* is a powerful diatribe that summarizes the injustices of the Spanish conquest throughout the New World. Its singlemindedness and exaggerations—the Indians are always portrayed as good natured, while the Spanish colonists introduce only evil—are explained by the fact that the work was written as a central part of Las Casas's political campaign to reform the Laws of the Indies. Its intention was not to present an impartial view of the conquest. A Humanist educated at the University of Salamanca, Las Casas began a major general history of the Indies which included numerous arguments to prove the excellence of pre-Columbian civilizations, but could not finish it. Another major anthropological study of all the Amerindian groups, entitled *Apologética historia sumaria*, was left unpublished.

Las Casas's polemical book effectively raised the issue of Indian rights in Spain. Much to his chagrin, though, the *Brevissima* was widely used by England and Holland as evidence of Spanish cruelty. This Protestant propaganda campaign against Spain and the Catholic Church became known as the "black legend." Some of the seventeenth-century English editions had this remarkable title: *Casas' horrid massacres, butcheries, and cruelties that hell and malice could invent committed by the Spaniards in the West Indies.*

44. *José de Acosta.* HISTORIA NATURAL Y MORAL DE LAS INDIAS. Seville, 1590.

Acosta (1540–1600) entered the Jesuit order at the age of fourteen and received a solid education in the humanities. In 1570 he went to Peru, where he taught theology at the Jesuit College in Lima and served as provincial of his order. After spending one more year in Mexico City, he returned to Spain with a considerable quantity of notes, many of them taken during his numerous travels. He organized and elaborated this material in a Latin work, entitled *De Natura Novi Orbis*, and then expanded it into his masterpiece, the *Historia*. As a natural historian, Acosta surpassed Oviedo. He took a philosophical approach to natural phenomena, searching for causes and effects in a spirit of critical inquiry. When experience contradicted Aristotelian theories, Acosta used reason to seek the truth. Acosta's attachment to scientific explanation devoid of reliance upon wonders and miracles, merited Von Humboldt's praise two centuries later. The subject of his moral history is pre-Columbian civilizations, particularly the Aztecs and the Incas, whose religions, customs, and governments he admiringly compares. Acosta reminded his readers that most aspects of Indian life that were perceived in a negative light by Europeans, including human sacrifices, also existed in the celebrated civilizations of Greece and Rome.

Acosta's *Historia* won him instant admiration in European academic circles. In Spain he was appointed rector of the Jesuit College of the University of Salamanca, and translations abroad surfaced quickly: in Italy in 1596, in France, Holland and Germany in 1598, and in England in 1604.

45. *Nicolás Monardes.* PRIMERA Y SEGUNDA Y TERCERA PARTES DE LA HISTORIA MEDICINAL. Seville, 1574.

Monardes (c. 1512–1588) was a distinguished physician based in Seville. Although he never went to the New World, he devoted his life to the collection and the study of specimens brought to him from the Americas with a purported medical value. The *Historia*, which instantly became a classic in the history of medicine, amounts to a true encyclopedia of the practical natural history of the area. Numerous plants and animals previously unknown to Europeans were described by Monardes for the first time. Some of the products discussed in detail are cocoa, sarsaparilla, and sassafras. The systematic description of all healing products is followed by the methods and the ways they are to be used, which in many cases are based upon Indian practices. Guaiac wood, for example, is presented as the Indian remedy for venereal disease. The long description of the healing uses of tobacco includes a reference to the Indians' unusual habit of lighting a dry leaf of tobacco in order to inhale its smoke "for to make theim selves drunk withall and to see the visions, and things that doe represent to them, wherein thei doe delight."

This is the first complete edition of Monardes's work, several parts of which were published separately before. Translations soon appeared in Latin, Italian, French, and English printings. In the first English edition, translated by Peter Frampton, authorship was wrongfully credited to García d'Orta, a Portuguese physician who prepared a similar work to that of Monardes on Far East products. It was published in London in 1577 with a long title but usually referred to as *Joyfull newes out of the newe founde world*. It was reprinted in 1580 and 1596 with proper attribution to Monardes.

46. *Antonio de Herrera y Tordesillas.* HISTORIA GENERAL DE LOS HECHOS DE LOS CASTELLANOS EN LAS ISLAS I TIERRA FIRME DEL MAR OCEANO. Madrid, 1601–1615.

Herrera (d. 1625) served as secretary to the viceroy Gonzaga in Naples and Navarre until 1586, when he was appointed by King Philip II as Cronista Mayor de Indias, a post he held until his death. Herrera was an accomplished historian who also wrote histories of France, Portugal, Scotland, and England. The *Historia* is a huge work of erudition. Its author, who never crossed the Atlantic Ocean, incorporated the greatest collection of sources up to that date, including many important writings that had not yet been published, such as the histories of Bernal Díaz and Bartolomé de las Casas, and the valuable *Geografía y descripción universal de las Indias* by the cosmographer Juan López de Velasco. Written in a rather dry style, the four volumes of the *Historia* may be faulted for giving little attention to Indian ethnography, but they constitute a true encyclopedia of all the facts pertaining to the Spanish in-

FIGURE 25. Antonio de Herrera y Tordesillas. *Historia general de los hechos de los castellanos.* Madrid, 1601–1615. The title page of Herrera's Fifth Decade contains portraits of thirteen pre-Hispanic Inca rulers.

volvement with the Indies between 1492 and 1555. The narrated events are arranged in chronological order by decades. Since the author was sufficiently removed from the facts he narrated, he made judgments without worrying about posssible accusations and lawsuits by the people involved, a common problem in many of the earlier histories of the Indies.

The *Historia*'s unique wealth of information made it, from the moment of its appearance, an indispensable work of reference on the subject. In Spain it was soon reprinted. A French translation was published in Paris between 1660 and 1671. The earliest English edition appeared in six volumes in London in 1725–1726.

47. *Bernardo de Vargas Machuca*. MILICIA Y DESCRIPCION DE LAS INDIAS.
    Madrid, 1599.

Vargas Machuca (1557–1622) had a distinguished military career in the Spanish army. After serving in Spain and Italy, he fought the Indians from New Granada to Chile, ascending to the rank of captain general of Peru. In response to a request by the Council of the Indies for a report on the best means by which to conquer and colonize Chile, where numerous rebellions had taken place, Vargas undertook instead to write a truly unique book whose subject was the military organization of the Indies. The purpose of the book was mostly practical. Vargas used his long experience to provide useful information for Europeans who were planning to go to the New World. Written in the manner of a modern guide, the *Milicia* contains interesting advice on how to adapt to both the natural environment and the psychology of the Indians, and its recommendations are frequently illustrated with instances drawn from his own experience. There are discussions of climatic conditions, edible products, animals and insects, common health problems, and the best way to make peace and war with the Indians. A useful glossary of New World vocabulary is also included at the end.

No reprints or translations of the *Milicia* appeared until a modern edition in Spanish was published in Madrid in 1892. The work has lately drawn increasing critical attention from scholars.

48. *Juan de Solórzano Pereira*. DISPUTATIONEM DE INDIARUM JURE.
    Madrid, 1629–1639.

Solórzano (1575–1655) was born in Madrid. He studied Law at Salamanca and became professor of that University at the age of twenty-four. His expertise in legal matters won him an appointment as Oidor of the Audiencia in Lima in 1610, and upon return to Spain in 1626, as an officer in the Council of the Indies. A learned man, familiar with the Classics, as well as Roman, Canon, and Castillian Law, Solórzano compiled and studied all the royal decrees and laws pertaining to the New World. The *Disputationem*, written in elegant Latin prose,

FIGURE 26. Bernardo de Vargas Machuca. *Milicia y descripcion de las Indias.* Madrid, 1599. The Spaniard on the title page calls for further exploration and conquest of the American continent: "With the sword and the compass—more and more and more and more."

is an extraordinarily erudite legal history of the Indies, divided into five books. Book I, which serves as a general introduction to the rest, is a political and military history of the discovery, acquisition, and retention of the Indies. Books II and III deal with the political and legal status of the Indians, including a thorough study of the *encomienda* system. Book IV is dedicated to all church institutions in the New World. Book V analyzes the political organi-

FIGURE 27. Juan de Solórzano Pereira. *Disputationem de Indiarum jure.* Madrid, 1629–1639. King Philip IV, flanked by Spain and America, rules his world.

zation of the Indies, from local governments to the Viceroyalty and the Supreme Council of the Indies. Far from being a mere compiler, Solórzano fearlessly advances his own opinions and recommendations on most issues, particularly on things concerning the proper relation between Spaniards and Indians.

Solórzano's work was justifiably praised in all of Europe and the New World as the most important study ever undertaken on the historical projection of Spanish law in the Indies. Because of its thorough indexes, it became the indispensable reference book for both church and state officials. A compendium in Spanish, with the title *Política indiana* (Madrid, 1648), added a sixth book dealing with the complex tax system, which was a ground-breaking study of the subject.

## VII · *Church History*

THE SPANISH CATHOLIC CHURCH played a pivotal role in Spain's involvement with the New World. Pope Alexander VI had justified the conquest as a missionary enterprise, so authorities made sure that priests and friars accompanied each expedition, however small. Their immediate role, of course, was to spread the Christian faith. Once the Spanish had settled in the land, the friars were responsible not only for the Indians' religious indoctrination, but for their general education in Western ways as well. As their work progressed, the close contact with the Indian population in parishes, schools, and colleges allowed them to learn about native languages and cultures (see Chapter III above). Their work in this field was indeed impressive. Their efforts produced not only dictionaries and grammars of many Amerindian languages, but also catechisms and other books of indoctrination written and published in those tongues. Since not a few of these languages eventually died out, such works by missionaries and priests have become invaluable in preserving our knowledge of the range of Indian languages. Frequently the friars also assumed a leading role in the defense of Indian rights against abuses by laymen, a role accepted and even promoted by the state, which consistently sought to maintain a balance of power in the distant lands.

As direct witnesses of the conquest and as students of Indian cultures, a significant group of sixteenth-century historians of the New World were men who belonged to religious orders. This prominence increased even more in the next century, when, once the era of discoveries and conquests had come to an end, churchmen's accounts dominated historical writings about the New World. In Catholic countries like Spain and Italy, the triumph of the Counter Reformation brought about artistic and literary splendor, but the genre of historiography was overwhelmed by religious propaganda. The new spirit of the times called for history to serve the interests of the church, and as a result explanations that relied heavily on direct providential intervention were favored over critical approaches to the causes of events, and local histories were favored over general histories. In the seventeenth century the quality of historiography by churchmen generally declined.

Yet, the number of published historical works about the New World rose sharply. This remarkable editorial frenzy was caused by the intense competition among the various religious orders to promote and publicize their missionary work overseas. Mercedarians, Franciscans, Dominicans, Augustinians, and Jesuits financed the continuous publication of histories of their own religious provinces so as to prove their merit in protecting the spiritual and material welfare of the Indians. Their main value lies in the ethnographic information they provide on the Indian peoples before and after the conquest, on their original cultures as well as on the processes of acculturation. In that respect they are a veritable mine of data for today's historians, linguists, and anthropologists.

49. *Agustín Dávila Padilla*. HISTORIA DE LA FUNDACION Y DISCURSO DE LA PROVINCIA DE SANTIAGO DE MEXICO, DE LA ORDEN DE PREDICADORES. Madrid, 1596.

Dávila (1562–1604) was born in Mexico City into a family of conquistadors. He became a Dominican and taught philosophy and theology in Puebla and Mexico City. After a stay in Madrid and elsewhere in Europe he was appointed archbishop of Santo Domingo. There his order commissioned him to bring to completion a history of the Dominicans in Mexico that had been started by his fellow friar Andrés de Moguer. It covers the period from 1526, when the first Dominicans, headed by Domingo de Betanzos, arrived in New Spain, to 1590. The *Historia*, one of the earliest works of its kind, already has the typical dual structure that characterizes the genre: it contains a long chronological narrative of the foundation of the various provinces, followed by individual biographies of the most distinguished members of the order—in Dávila's work there are two long biographies of Betanzos and Bartolomé de Las Casas. In both parts, numerous miracles and wonders, narrated in detail, help illustrate both the role of providence and the great service rendered to Christianity. The tone throughout the whole work is correspondingly lofty and often enthusiastic.

50. *Juan de Torquemada*. MONARQUIA YNDIANA. Seville, 1615.

Torquemada (*c.* 1557–1664) was a Franciscan and head of his order's Mexico Province. The *Monarquía* is an ambitious work in three volumes covering the civilian and religious history of Mexico from pre-Columbian times to the end of the sixteenth century. It was largely based on the work of his fellow Franciscan Jerónimo de Mendieta's *Historia eclesiástica indiana*, which was not published probably because of its stern criticism of the colonists' abuses of the Indians. While tempering Mendieta's criticism, Torquemada basically reiterated his master's apocalyptic view of Mexico, according to which ancient Mexico, which he describes in detail, is compared with the captivity of the Jewish people in ancient Egypt, and Cortés is seen as a new David allowed by God to destroy the Mexican empire because of its idolatry and human sacrifices. The arrival of the Franciscans into New Spain is interpreted as the start of a new era, but political upheaval brings about a period of conflict, decadence, and plagues in the second half of the sixteenth century, similar to the fall of Babylon. Finally a new golden age of Christianity is foreseen in the future of New Spain, under the spiritual guidance of the Franciscans.

51. *Antonio de Remesal.* HISTORIA GENERAL DE LAS INDIAS OCIDENTALES, Y PARTICULAR DE LA GOVERNACION DE CHIAPA Y GUATEMALA. Madrid, 1620.

Remesal (b. *c.* 1570) was born in Galicia, in northwest Spain, to a noble family. He studied Classical languages in Salamanca, and in 1593 he entered the Dominican order. In 1613, after earning a doctorate in theology, Remesal sailed for the New World. He settled at the Convent of Santiago de los Caballeros in Guatemala, where he completed his research for the *Historia*. This well-documented work, divided into eleven parts, is the first civil and religious history of Central America. It starts with a narrative of the conquest of the territory and the founding of Santiago by Pedro de Alvarado, who was sent there by Hernán Cortés and became the first governor of Guatemala. Remesal then focuses on the history of the church, especially of his own Dominican order, but he also provides a useful summary of the most relevant political events. A fervent admirer of Father Las Casas, a fellow Dominican, Remesal dwells extensively on his legacy and his accomplishments as bishop of Chiapas and, like Las Casas, he is an ardent defender of the Indians' virtues while denouncing their frequent abuse by Spanish civilians. This attitude gained him much criticism from the local authorities and settlers in Mexico.

52. *Juan de Grijalva.* CRÓNICA DE LA ORDEN DE N.P.S. AUGUSTÍN EN LAS PROVINCIAS DE LA NUEVA ESPAÑA. Mexico, 1624.

Grijalva (1580–1638) was a mestizo from Colima, Mexico. After entering the Augustinian order he earned a doctorate in theology from the University of Mexico, and served as rector of the San Pablo College and as prior at the University of San Agustín in Mexico City. The *Crónica*, apparently written in less than two years, is the first historical work on the Augus-

FIGURE 28. Juan de Torquemada. *Monarchia yndiana*. Seville, 1615. A Franciscan friar teaches the Christian doctrine to Mexican Indian men and women, apparently making use of graphic depictions.

tinian order in the New World. It is divided into four parts. The first deals with the arrival of the first friars in 1533 and their dispersion throughout New Spain. The second part tells of the constitution of the province of Mexico and contains an informative narrative on the methods and ways used to convert the Indians, with pertinent discussion of the results. The third part tells of the founding of San Pablo College and of the missionary work among the Tarascan Indians, culminating in the establishment of the Michoacan province. As was customary, the *Crónica* ends with a series of biographies of the most prominent members of the order written in a laudatory tone. Later chroniclers of other Augustinian provinces used Grijalva as their model.

53. *Juan Meléndez*. TESOROS VERDADEROS DE LAS YNDIAS EN LA HISTORIA DE LA GRAN PROVINCIA DE SAN JUAN BAUTISTA DEL PERÚ. Rome, 1681–1682.

Meléndez (*fl.* 1681) was born in Lima. He became a Dominican priest and went on to acquire a doctorate in theology and philosophy. He taught and held prominent positions in several convents, becoming procurator of the Dominican province of Peru in 1671. Two years later he was sent to Madrid and then to Rome, where he completed and published his voluminous book. A strongly partisan author, Meléndez's clear objective was to give his order the honor of providing the first Christian preachers in Peru, against similar claims by other rival orders. But in his three-volume *Tesoros* he also gives a highly erudite account of the conquest of Peru, and he incorporates significant information about Inca religious practices and a famous description of colonial life in seventeenth-century Lima, both taken from Francisco Antonio Montalvo's unpublished manuscript *El sol del Nuevo Mundo*. The third volume of his work is entirely dedicated to biographies of distinguished Dominicans in Peru, including one on Martín de Porres, who became the first Peruvian man designated as a saint. Meléndez's concise style has been praised as a rarity among his contemporaries, who usually prefered the complicated syntax typical of the Baroque period.

54. *Antonio de la Calancha*. CORONICA MORALIZADA DEL ORDEN DE SAN AUGUSTIN EN EL PERU. Barcelona, 1639.

Calancha (1584–1654) was a creole from La Plata (today's Sucre, in Bolivia). At the age of fourteen he entered the Augustinian order. He earned a doctorate at the University of San Marcos in Lima and went on to become a famous preacher while holding the highest positions in the Peruvian convents of his order. In his numerous travels throughout the country, which he never left, Calancha collected archaeological, ethnographic, historical, astrological, and natural information. He used all of this material, plus many written sources, for his

FIGURE 29. Juan Meléndez. *Tesoros verdaderos de las Yndias en la historia de la gran provincia de San Juan Bautista del Perú*. Rome, 1681–1682. This title page honors the earliest and most prominent Dominican friars in Peru. Also shown are Emperor Charles V, Francisco Pizarro, and Rosa de Lima, the first woman in the New World to attain sainthood.

FIGURE 30. Juan Meléndez. *Tesoros verdaderos de las Yndias en la historia de la gran provincia de San Juan Bautista del Perú*. Rome, 1681–1682. A Dominican convent in Lima, Peru.

*Corónica*, a work of considerable value for the study of seventeenth-century colonial life in spite of its abstruse Baroque style and loose structure. Particularly important are his writings on the history and the religion of the Peruvian coastal Indians, as well as his descriptions of all social strata of colonial life, both secular and religious. Calancha points out the particular ways in which Christian practices have accommodated themselves to the indigenous cul-

FIGURE 31. Antonio de la Calancha. *Coronica moralizada del orden de San Augustin en el Peru.* Barcelona, 1639.

FIGURE 32. Antonio de la Calancha. *Coronica moralizada del orden de San Augustin en el Peru.* Barcelona, 1639. An illustration of the martyrdom of the Augustinian Fr. Diego Ortiz by Peruvian Indians.

ture. In the case of the Indians, these practices are tainted by idolatry, and in the case of creoles marred by superstition. The second volume, left unfinished, was published posthumously by Bernardo de Torres, who added a biography of Calancha.

Calancha's work is one of the few historical writings about religion that was reedited in Spain and translated abroad, although in condensed versions. Extracts of Part I were published in Italian at Genoa in 1645, in Dutch at Antwerp in 1651, and in French at Toulouse in 1653 with the title *Histoire du Perou aux Antepodes*.

55. *Antonio Ruiz de Montoya*. CONQUISTA ESPIRITUAL HECHA POR LOS RELIGIOSOS DE LA COMPAÑIA DE JESUS, EN LAS PROVINCIAS DEL PARAGUAY, PARANA, URUGUAY, Y TAPE. Madrid, 1639.

Ruiz de Montoya (1558–1652) was born in Lima and entered the Jesuit Order in 1606. He spent most of his active life doing missionary work in Paraguay, where he served as head of the Jesuit Province between 1623 and 1637. Ruiz was recognized for his expertise in the Guaraní language, for which he wrote several dictionaries that were published in Spain and other countries. The *Conquista* is arguably the best narrative of the establishment of the famous *reducciones*, communities of Indians organized by the Jesuits in Paraguay as an alternative to the usual forms of village life, and thought to be more beneficial and protective of the Indians' welfare. Ruiz's history, which is largely autobiographical, is somewhat vague in its chronology and geographic data, but he provides unique descriptions of Indian customs and of the exchanges between Indians and Spaniards. Also recorded are numerous incidents with the Paulistas, the slave hunters who periodically raided Paraguay from their bases in Brazil.

# VIII · *Biography*

BIOGRAPHY is a modern genre if by this we mean a critical and independent assessment of someone's life, devoid of propagandistic purposes. In the sixteenth century, the notion of biography was still largely associated with hagiography, the exemplary narratives of the lives of saints, a genre that had a long tradition in Christian countries. That tradition, given new life by the spirit of the Counter Reformation, flourished in the seventeenth century and found particular application in works concerning the New World, since both the state and the church promoted the American enterprise as a new crusade whose main justification lay in the spreading of Christianity. As was earlier noted, many local church histories included biographies of those members of a religious order thought by the author to be the most prominent missionaries in a particular area. There were also works that consisted exclusively of a collection of biographies, all written in the customary tone of praise and containing numerous prodigies that attested to the exemplary character of their protagonists. And when the subject was so exceptional as to be worthy of beatification or sainthood, even a whole book was dedicated to the praise of his or her deeds.

The spirit of personal or group vindication was also responsible for a small group of biographies whose main goal was to exalt the deeds of prominent discoverers and conquistadors. The spirit of the Renaissance, with its new awareness of the individual, undoubtedly provided a good general foundation for the exaltation of personal achievement. There were also other more concrete reasons for the emergence of this new genre. As the protagonists were frequently the subject of controversy and official reprimand, the obvious goal of some biographies was to restore or upgrade someone's personal reputation as a contributor to the imperial enterprise. When the authors of such biographies were family relatives of their biographees, it is no surprise to find even legal and financial claims as the underlying reason behind these works.

56. *Francisco Jarque.* INSIGNES MISSIONEROS DE LA COMPAÑIA DE JESUS EN LA PROVINCIA DEL PARAGUAY. Pamplona, 1687.

Jarque (1609–1691) was born in Albarracín, Spain. He joined the Jesuit order and did extensive missionary work in Paraguay before an incurable illness incapacitated him for this task. He then acted as curate of Potosí and metropolitan judge in the archbishopric of Charcas, before returning to his hometown in Spain. Jarque prepared for his work by collecting extensive oral and written information on his order's activities in the province of Paraguay, which included the Paraguay, Tucumán, and Río de la Plata districts. He also had access to written documents, especially the long yearly reports sent from the Jesuit provinces to the superiors in Rome informing them of their activities. The work is divided into three books. The first two are long biographies of two prominent Jesuit missionaries, the Italian Simón Mazeta (1582–1658) and Francisco Díaz Taño (1593–1677), written in the customary laudatory tone and containing a rich collection of anecdotes of personal travails and achievements. The third book is a full account of the state of the Paraguay missions at the time. Some chapters provide excellent information on how an Indian "reduction" was formed, ruled, and sustained, and on all aspects concerning everyday life. Throughout his work, Jarque gave details not found elsewhere about the frequent incursions of the Portuguese, who claimed some of the Paraguay territory, and the clashes that ensued.

57. *Diego de Córdova Salinas.* VIDA, VIRTUDES, Y MILAGROS DEL APOSTOL DEL PERU EL B. P. FR. FRANCISCO SOLANO. Madrid, 1676.

The grandson of a conquistador, Córdova Salinas was born in Lima. Soon after entering the Franciscan order, he was commissioned to be its chronicler in Peru, and the *Vida* is his first work. Francisco Solano was one of the most distinguished Franciscan missionaries in Peru and soon after his death his order started a process of beatification. Córdova's brother, Buenaventura de Salinas y Córdova, also a Franciscan, was sent to Rome to present Solano's dossier at the Vatican. This was used by Córdova to write his biography, which is basically a rewritten version of the dossier, in order to make Solano's case better known among the general public. As the full title explains, the *Vida* incorporates the depositions of some five hundred witnesses who knew Solano.

58. *Jacinto de Parra.* ROSA LAUREADA ENTRE LOS SANTOS. Madrid, 1670.

Parra (17th cent.) was a Dominican who became head of the Convent of Santo Tomás in Madrid. Santa Rosa de Lima (1586–1627), who took her name because at the age of three her face was seen transformed into a rose, was the first woman born in the New World who attained sainthood. Parra's voluminous work of seven hundred-plus pages is a loosely organized compendium on Santa Rosa's virtues and deeds. It begins with a biographical portrait of the saint in which her numerous virtues are illustrated with concrete actions, giving the author an opportunity to constantly praise her in the highest rhetorical style of the Baroque period. Parra then provides an extensive account of the processes of beatification and canonization, including picturesque descriptions of the numerous festivities that took place in Madrid on both occasions. Also included in the volume are sermons preached by several priests, among them one by the Franciscan José de Mitares who knew Santa Rosa. Parra's work is clearly inferior to the famous biography written by Leonard Hansen (published in 1664), which was a best-seller throughout Europe and has since become a truly rare book.

59. *Fernando Pizarro y Orellana.* VARONES ILUSTRES DEL NUEVO MUNDO. Madrid, 1639.

Pizarro (d. 1652?) was a great grandson of Francisco Pizarro. He was also born in Trujillo (Extremadura, Spain), but unlike his famous ancestor, he was a man of letters who never went to the New World. Instead, he remained in Spain and had a notable political career, holding office in the Supreme Council of Castile. The civil wars in Peru had for a long time tarnished the reputation of the Pizarro family—Gonzalo had even been charged with treason—obscuring their achievements as conquistadors. Clearly, Pizarro y Orellano's partisan objective in writing the lives of his ancestors Francisco, Juan, and Gonzalo Pizarro was to defend and praise their actions, and ultimately lay claim to several grants and rights due their descendants. In order to hide this intention he cleverly included in his work biographies of other prominent discoverers such as Columbus, who by then was almost forgotten, Hernán Cortés, Alonso de Ojeda, and Diego García de Paredes. All the biographies are written in the same elevated tone of admiration, the narration being constantly enhanced with numerous erudite notes and comments in which the deeds of the subjects are favorably compared to those achieved by the great heroes of antiquity. In sharp contrast to the others, the biography of Diego de Almagro, the Pizarristas' great foe during the civil wars, is characterized by a poorly disguised tone of condemnation, his actions being shown as the tragic result of his personal shortcomings.

60. *Fernando Colón.* HISTORIE ... DELLA VITA, & DE'FATTI DELL'AMMIRAGLIO D. CHRISTOFORO COLOMBO, SUO PADRE. Venice, 1571.

Colón (1488–1539), an illegitimate son of Columbus and Beatriz Enríquez de Arana, was born in Córdoba, Spain. As a young man he accompanied his father on his fourth trip to the New World, but he never returned there. Instead, during most of his life he traveled incessantly throughout Europe as a courtier of Charles V before retiring in Seville. The reputation of Columbus had significantly faded after his death—some authors even denied he was the rightful discoverer of the Indies—but Colón kept up efforts to recover the royal grants and privileges claimed by his father. In this context, he set upon the writing of a biography of the Admiral which would set the record straight and establish him as a great historical figure. Colón had access to all the family papers and Columbus's annotated books, which he himself had collected, including the now lost *Diario*, but the availability of this material did not make him an accurate or an objective biographer. Not infrequently, dates and places given are wrong, and Columbus is systematically praised as an indefatigable man of genius and virtue, devoid of any defects, while his collaborators are omitted and his detractors strongly condemned. Colón's positive portrait of his father was the basis for Washington Irving's celebrated biography of Columbus.

The original manuscript of Colón's work, written in Spanish, was taken to Italy. There it was lost, but an Italian translation by Alfonso Ulloa was preserved and published in Venice. For many years critics disputed its authenticity, but modern scholars now believe the *Historie* was undoubtedly written by Columbus's son. An early English translation appeared in 1604.

FIGURE 33. Fernando Colón. *Historie . . . della vita, & de' fatti dell'ammiraglio D. Christoforo Colombo*. Venice, 1571.

61. *Cristóbal Suárez de Figueroa*. HECHOS DE DON GARCIA HURTADO DE MENDOZA, QUARTO MARQUES DE CAÑETE. Madrid, 1613.

Suárez (*c.* 1571–1645), was born in Valladolid, Spain. He was a learned man, who held several high positions in Spain and Italy, and a prolific author of several literary works in both poetry and prose. Suárez was commissioned to write this biography of Don García (1535–1609) by Juan Andrés Hurtado de Mendoza, García's son and heir, with the declared intent of praising the memory of his recently deceased father, who had been viceroy of Peru. Suárez never went to the Indies—he actually despised them—and he did not know his biographee

FIGURE 34. Alonso de Ovalle. *Historica relacion*. Rome, 1646. A portrait of Governor García Hurtado de Mendoza.

personally, but he had access to the family's archives and to a manuscript copy of an unpublished chronicle by Pedro Mariño de Lobera. The latter, although a highly unreliable work, constituted Suárez's main source of information. All seven chapters of the book underline the services to the crown rendered by Don García in the New World, and he is consequently portrayed as an exemplary military commander and civilian leader. In the final chapter of the book, an undeclared purpose for writing the biography becomes apparent. Suárez states that Don García was about to receive important royal favors for his services when the untimely death of the monarch prevented this from happening. A firm request to grant the favors due to Don García's son, Juan Andrés, is then made explicit.

## IX · *Literature*

SCHOLARS have long disputed about the relationship between historical writing and literature. Although poetry is by definition a genre based on principles quite different from those governing historiography, epic poems since Homer represent a particular subgenre in which many features of both genres meet. To be sure, an epic poet may deliberately suppress, invent, or significantly alter the facts, an artistic freedom denied to the historian, but personal perspectives and interpretations have also played a role in historical writing, and were certainly in evidence in writing about the New World. The same could be argued about the elevated tone of praise characteristic of epic poems, which was equally prevalent in many chronicles discussed in the preceding chapters. Their authors sought precisely to address a general public too distant or incredulous to appreciate the true epic proportions of the American enterprise. These common interests of the two genres make the modern distinction between them a tenuous one. It is undeniable that in their time many epic poems were written and read as historical works.

After enjoying an epoch of splendor in the early Middle Ages, epic poetry steadily declined in Europe—even though it theoretically still retained the privileged position it had been given in Aristotelian poetics—until it was revived in Italy by Ludovico Ariosto and Torquato Tasso. In Spain, it had lay dormant for several centuries before the genre surprisingly staged a comeback in the second half of the sixteenth century and knew an era of unusual popularity. Undoubtedly, the discovery of the New World was the key reason for this revival, for it was largely stimulated by the publication of Alonso de Ercilla's *La Araucana*, the first epic poem about the New World. Ercilla's poem, which deals with the conquest of Chile and is unanimously regarded as the best and the most influential epic poem in the

Spanish Golden Age, incorporated into epic poetry the proud awareness of the conquistadors' contribution to the Spanish imperial enterprise, a theme prevalent in the chronicles.

The particular difficulty of the conquest of Chile made this a most favored subject of epic poets, six of whom wrote works on the subject. Also popular were the conquest of Mexico, whose main protagonist, Hernán Cortés, quickly acquired in Europe the legendary status of a Renaissance hero, and the conquest of Peru.

62. *Alonso de Ercilla y Zúñiga*. LA ARAUCANA. Madrid, 1569.

Ercilla (1533–1594) was a well-educated courtier when, at the age of twenty-one, he accompanied Don García Hurtado de Mendoza, the newly appointed viceroy of Peru, to America. He participated as a soldier in the wars against the Araucanian Indians of Chile, who had staged a rebellion against Spanish rule. This is the subject of *La Araucana*, a poem divided into three parts. The first part is a sympathetic history of the Araucanos and their success in retaining their independence throughout the years, in which Ercilla portrays them as dignified and bellicose in the heroic defense of their freedom. The other two books deal mostly with their battles against the Spaniards until their final defeat. Although Ercilla based his poem on actual facts, he also made frequent reference to unusual, extraordinary, and even absurd events (all of which was allowed by the conventions of that genre) as well as divine intervention. Thanks to his effective language, full of images and powerful comparisons, Ercilla succeeded in his intention of elevating a local rebellion in a remote location in South America into the epic confrontation of two nations.

This is the first printed edition of Part One of *La Araucana*. Part Two was first published in 1578, and Part Three in 1589, both in Madrid. The first complete edition, including all three parts, appeared in Madrid in 1590.

63. *Pedro de Oña*. ARAUCO DOMADO. Lima, 1596.

The son of a conquistador, Oña (1570?–1643?) was born in Chile and studied arts and theology at the University of San Marcos in Lima. He was commissioned by Don Diego Hurtado de Mendoza's family to write this poem, one aim of which was to improve upon Don Diego's portrayal in *La Araucana*. After having had some serious differences with Don Diego, Ercilla had been condemned to death by him, a sentence later commuted to permanent exile. Ercilla took literary revenge by stressing the heroic behavior of the Araucanos while criticizing and obscuring the role of Don Diego, the commander of the Spanish army. After the tremendous success of *La Araucana*, Oña set out to rewrite the epic history of the Arauco wars emphasizing the role of Don Diego, who becomes the sole and distinguished

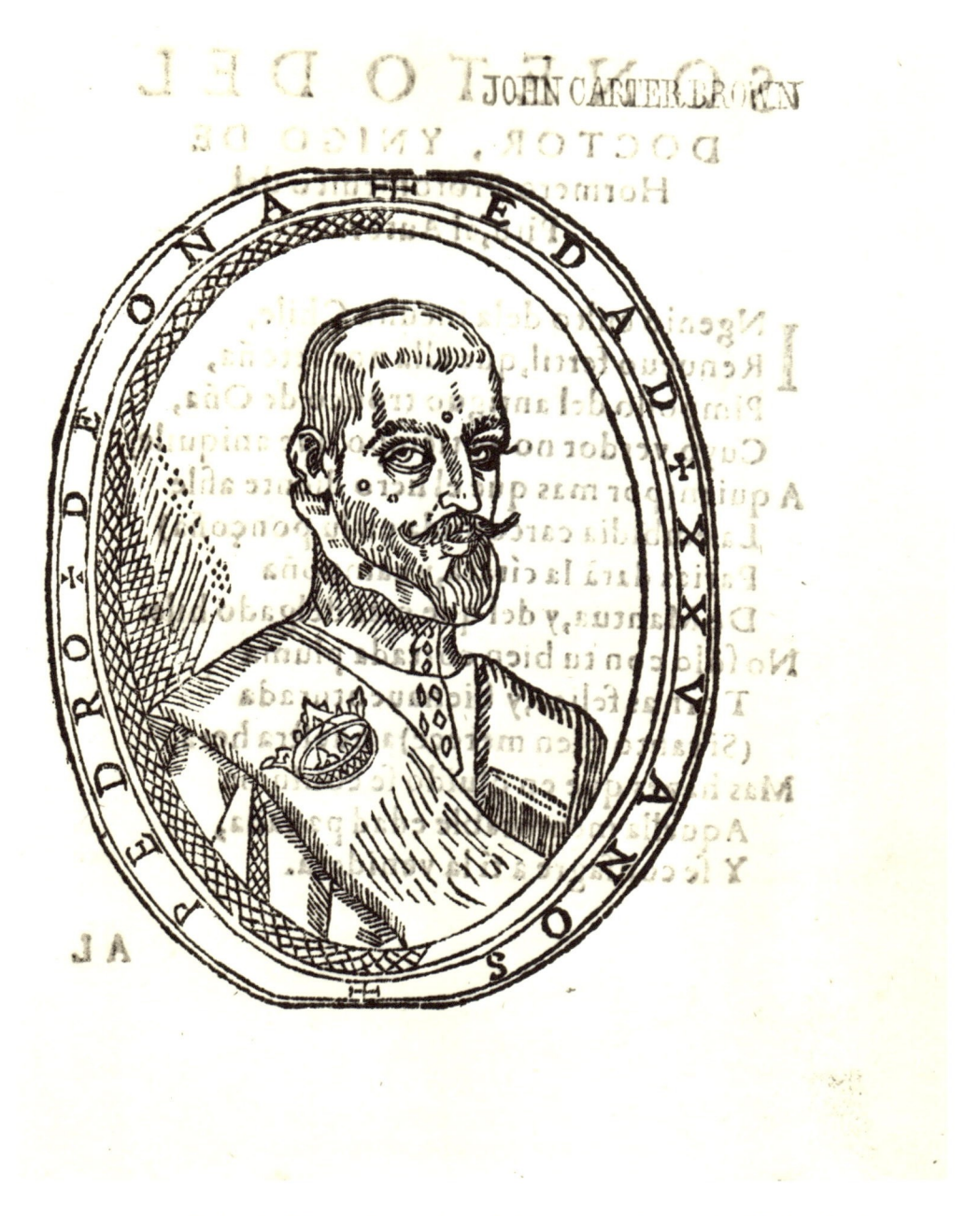

FIGURE 35. Pedro de Oña. *Arauco domado*. Lima, 1596. A portrait of Pedro de Oña.

protagonist of his poem. He is portrayed as the exemplary leader of an army which embodies all the political and the religious ideals of the Spanish Empire, whereas the Araucanos are depicted as the uncivilized pagans who by providential design are punished for their sinful and hedonistic lifestyle.

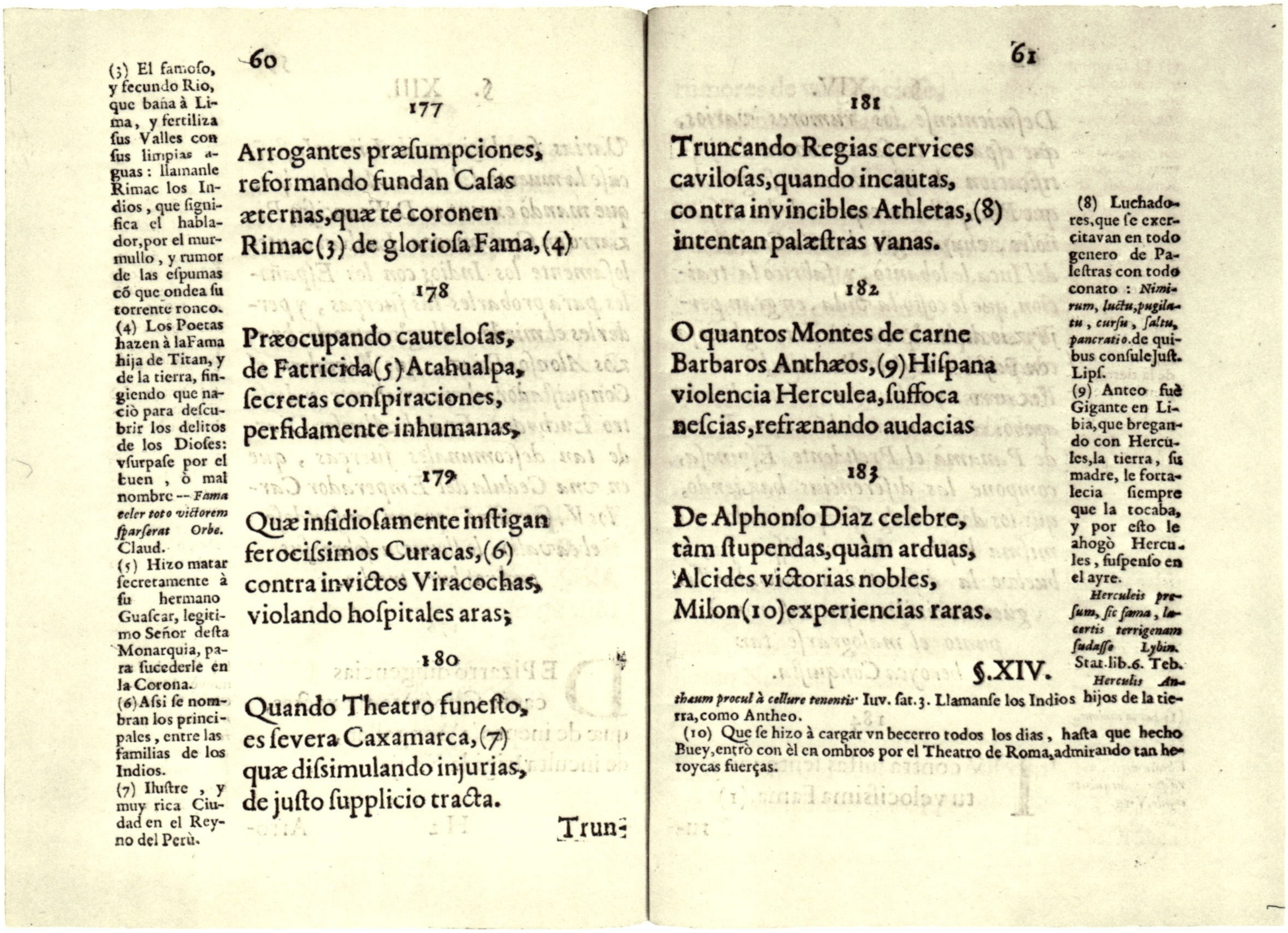

60

177

Arrogantes præſumpciones,
reformando fundan Caſas
æternas,quæ te coronen
Rimac(3) de glorioſa Fama,(4)

178

Præocupando cauteloſas,
de Fatricida(5) Atahualpa,
ſecretas conſpiraciones,
perfidamente inhumanas,

179

Quæ inſidioſamente inſtigan
ferocisſimos Curacas,(6)
contra invictos Viracochas,
violando hoſpitales aras;

180

Quando Theatro funeſto,
es ſevera Caxamarca,(7)
quæ diſsimulando injurias,
de juſto ſupplicio tracta.

Trun-

(3) El famoſo, y fecundo Rio, que baña à Lima, y fertiliza ſus Valles con ſus limpias aguas: llamanle Rimac los Indios, que ſignifica el hablador, por el murmullo, y rumor de las eſpumas cõ que ondea ſu torrente ronco.

(4) Los Poetas hazen à la Fama hija de Titan, y de la tierra, fingiendo que naciò para deſcubrir los delitos de los Dioſes: vſurpaſe por el buen, ò mal nombre -- *Fama celer toto victorem ſparſerat Orbe.* Claud.

(5) Hizo matar ſecretamente à ſu hermano Guaſcar, legitimo Señor deſta Monarquia, para ſucederle en la Corona.

(6) Aſsi ſe nombran los principales, entre las familias de los Indios.

(7) Iluſtre, y muy rica Ciudad en el Reyno del Perù.

61

181

Truncando Regias cervices
caviloſas, quando incautas,
contra invincibles Athletas,(8)
intentan palæſtras vanas.

182

O quantos Montes de carne
Barbaros Anthæos,(9) Hiſpana
violencia Herculea, ſuffoca
neſcias, refrænando audacias

183

De Alphonſo Diaz celebre,
tàm ſtupendas, quàm arduas,
Alcides victorias nobles,
Milon(10) experiencias raras.

§.XIV.

(8) Luchadores, que ſe excercitavan en todo genero de Paleſtras con todo conato: *Nimirum, luctu, pugilatu, curſu, ſaltu, pancratio.* de quibus conſule Juſt. Lipſ.

(9) Anteo fuè Gigante en Libia, que bregando con Hercules, la tierra, ſu madre, le fortalecia ſiempre que la tocaba, y por eſto le ahogò Hercules, ſuſpenſo en el ayre. *Herculeis preſſum, ſic fama, lacertis terrigenam ſudaſſe Lybim.* Stat. lib. 6. Teb. *Herculis Anthaum procul à cellure tenentis* Iuv. ſat. 3. Llamanſe los Indios hijos de la tierra, como Antheo.

(10) Que ſe hizo à cargar vn becerro todos los dias, haſta que hecho Buey, entrò con èl en ombros por el Theatro de Roma, admirando tan heroycas fuerças.

FIGURE 36. Rodrigo de Valdés. *Poema heroyco hispano-latino panegyrico.* Madrid, 1687. The stanzas of this poem are written in a way that can be read both as Latin and as Spanish.

64. *Rodrigo de Valdés.* POEMA HEROYCO HISPANO-LATINO PANEGYRICO DE LA FUNDACION, Y GRANDEZAS DE LA MUY NOBLE Y LEAL CIUDAD DE LIMA. Madrid, 1687.

Valdés (1609–1682) was a Jesuit born and educated in Lima. He was professor of theology and director of studies at the Jesuit College of San Pablo in Lima. His *Poema heroyco* is a long poem of five hundred and seventy-two four-line stanzas. The adjective "hispano-latino" in its title refers to its highly unusual linguistic character. Responding to a Baroque fashion that applauded artistic wit, the poem is written in a language that can be read both as

Latin and as Spanish. In his dedication to King Charles II, the editor of the poem, Francisco Garabito de León, the author's nephew, states that the author's purpose was to write a useful book for the study of the Latin language, by singling out cognates between that language and Spanish. The poetic merit of Valdés's work is dubious at best, but the *Poema* sheds light on many aspects of the founding of Lima, including descriptions of convents, palaces, and other buildings, such as the Casa de la Moneda (Royal Mint) in Lima, streets, bridges, and the natural products of the region. It also provides vivid descriptions of events, such as processions, the christening of a galleon, and some historic scenes pertaining to the conquest of Peru. The poem ends with praise of the local saint, Rosa de Lima. According to its editor, the author of the *Poema* tore the manuscript into many pieces on his deathbed, but it was rescued and put back together by an admiring fellow friar.

65. *Gaspar Pérez de Villagrá.* HISTORIA DE LA NUEVA MÉXICO.
Alcalá de Henares, 1610.

Villagrá (d. 1620) was born to a family of illustrious captains in Puebla, Mexico. He went to Spain and graduated as bachelor of letters from the University of Salamanca. In 1595, soon after returning to New Spain, he enlisted in Juan de Oñate's expedition to New Mexico, in which Villagrá played a major role as one of its captains. His poem is a true history of the conquest of New Mexico in thirty-four cantos for which Villagrá used both documents and his own recollections as sources. The *Historia* starts with a description of the land and a narration of early expeditions, including Fr. Marcos de Niza's account of the fabulous Seven Cities of Cibola and the ensuing expedition commanded by Francisco Vázquez de Coronado. Villagrá then narrates in detail the most important events that befell Oñate's expedition, ending with the battle of Acoma in 1599. Villagrá's merits as a poet are few indeed, but the historical value of his poem is indisputable. It provides not only the earliest and most accurate information on Spanish expeditions to New Mexico, but also unique information on the Pueblo Indians not found anywhere else. Villagrá's work is the first printed history of any territory now belonging to the United States.

66. *Gabriel Lasso de la Vega.* CORTÉS VALEROSO, Y MEXICANA. Madrid, 1588.

Lasso de la Vega (1559–*c.* 1615) was born in Madrid. He served as a soldier in France and Italy before settling in Madrid, where he gained a certain stature as a poet. Lasso's poem seems to have originated from a genuine admiration of Cortés, but as he himself declares in his foreword, both Martín Cortés, son of the conquistador, and Martín's son, Fernando, were involved in the project, perhaps as financial sponsors. *Mexicana* is a long epic poem divided into twenty-five cantos. It starts with the sailing of the fleet from Cuba to Yucatan, and ends

FIGURE 37. Gabriel Lasso de la Vega. *Cortés valeroso, y Mexicana*. Madrid, 1588. A portrait of Hernán Cortés at sixty-three years of age, with his coat of arms.

with the preparation of the Spanish army for the final siege of Tenochtitlan. A second part that would complete his work is announced at the end, but there is no record that it was ever written. Lasso draws from Gómara (see No. 9) both as a general source and in his portrayal of Cortés in particular, whom he presents as a hero singled out by God to carry out a providential mission to expand Christianity. Although highly hyperbolic in his praise of Cortés's actions, Lasso's poem remains close to the facts. At times, however, a curious mixture of fact and fiction typical of the genre occurs. Cortés's determination, for instance, prevails not only over the Mexicans, but also their allies Pluto, Neptune, and other ancient mythical gods who plot against him.

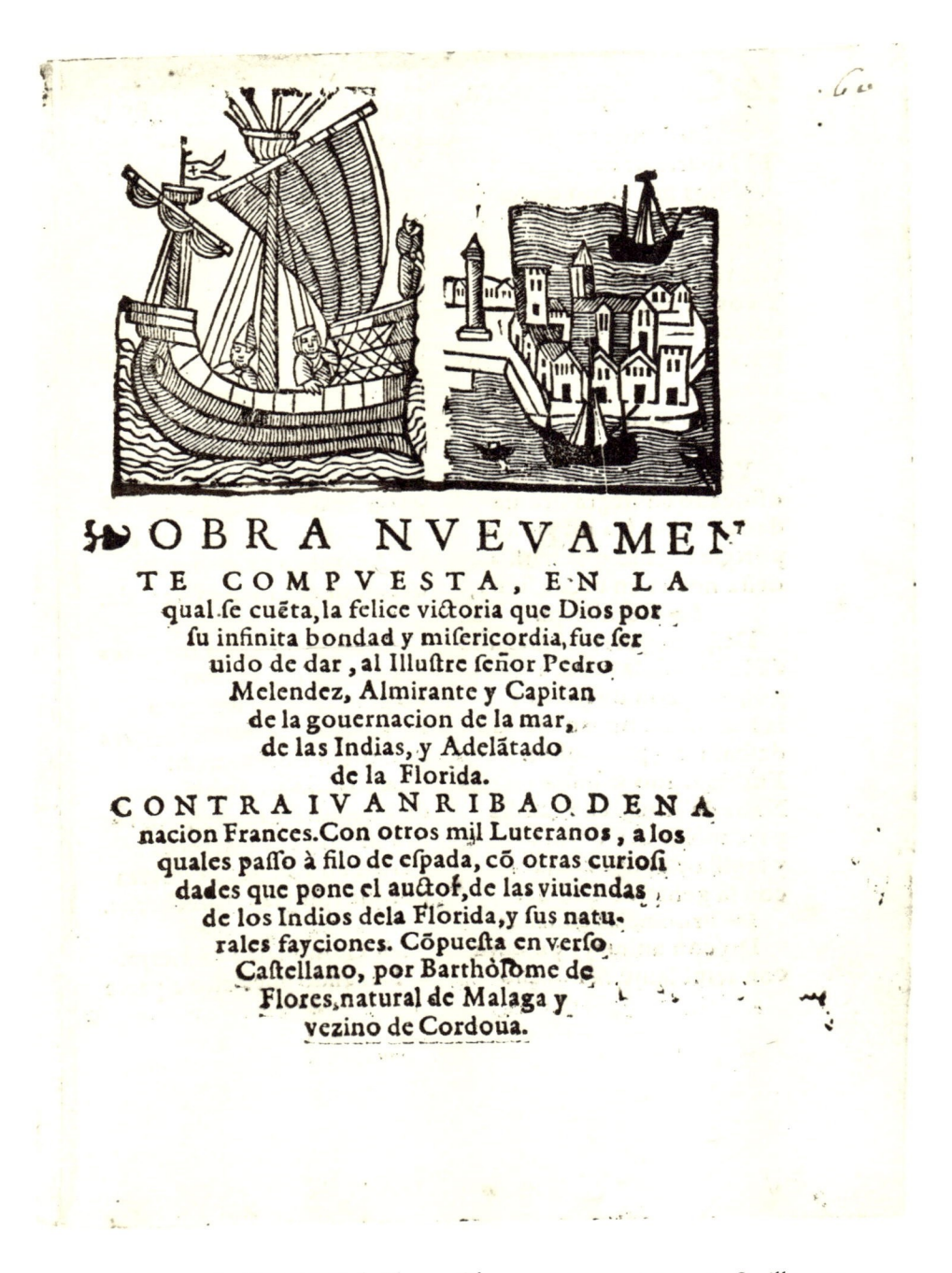

FIGURE 38. Bartolomé de Flores. *Obra nuevamente compuesta.* Seville, 1571.

67. *Bartolomé de Flores.* OBRA NUEVAMENTE COMPUESTA. Seville, 1571.

By the mid-sixteenth century the French were interested in settling in the southeast of North America, which as a whole was commonly called Florida. The French aim was to look for riches in the interior—the elusive Fountain of Youth and the Seven Cities of Cibola still fired the imagination of Europeans—and to be in a position to raid the Spanish fleets loaded with bullion. In 1564, the Huguenot captain René de Laudonnière founded Fort Caroline on the Saint John's River, in today's South Carolina. Upon learning of its existence, the Spanish lost no time in sending a punitive expedition from the newly settled colony of St. Augustine, led by Pedro Menéndez de Avilés, which attacked and destroyed Fort Caroline in 1565. This event is exalted in this poem by Flores (of whom nothing is known other than that he was born in Málaga and lived in Córdoba) as an act of divine punishment against the Calvinists. The 375-line poem ends with a detailed description of the land and its native people in which Florida, depicted as a natural paradise of rare beauty and abundance, is called the New Valencia. This hyperbole attests to the propagandistic nature of the *Obra*, whose underlying purpose doubtless was to recruit enthusiastic settlers for Menéndez's colonizing enterprise in what proved to be a rather harsh and hostile territory.

68. *Martín del Barco Centenera.* ARGENTINA Y CONQUISTA DEL RIO DE LA PLATA. Lisbon, 1602.

Barco (b. 1535) was born in Logrosán, a small town in Extremadura, Spain. He claims to have received a formal education in Salamanca. In 1572 he went to the New World and remained there for over twenty years, serving as a priest in a number of places in South America, his reputation being tainted by frequent accusations of living a dissipated life. Barco's poem, written as an imitation of Ercilla's *La Araucana* and divided into twenty-eight cantos, is a poorly organized account narrating his own experience in the Río de la Plata region. It provides useful data on the expeditions in which the author took part, especially the important ones commanded by Juan Ortiz de Zárate and Juan de Garay, the founder of Buenos Aires. Unfortunately, the narrative is marred by constant references to mythical places and fictional creatures which the author seems to accept with utter credulity. Literary historians agree on the practically non-existent literary value of the poem. Barco's major legacy was the name Argentina, which he created as a Latin adjective equivalent to the Spanish "platense" ("silvery") by which the land was known. Its constant use by Barco, who also included it in the title of the poem, gave it common currency, and it eventually became the name of the region and then the country.

69. *Juan de Castellanos.* ELEGÍAS DE VARONES ILLUSTRES DE INDIAS. Madrid, 1589.

Castellanos (1522–1607) was born in Alanís, Seville, and around 1540 he went to the New World. He began his career as a soldier, but in 1544 he became a priest and spent all his life serving as a parish priest in several places in New Granada. Castellanos may be considered the clearest example of a New World poet-chronicler, since he originally wrote a history in

FIGURE 39. Juan de Castellanos. *Elegías de varones illustres de Indias.* Madrid, 1589.

prose, but later decided to turn it into a long poem of over one hundred thousand lines, an enterprise that took him some fifteen years. The poem is a comprehensive history of New Granada divided into four parts. The first part, dealing with Columbus's travels and other early discoveries in the southern Caribbean region until the death of Lope de Aguirre, was the only one to attain publication during the author's lifetime, under the title *Elegies of illustrious men in the Indies*. Castellanos meant his work to be a poem of artistic merit and a chronicle of real historical value, and he takes pride in his having consulted extensive sources, both written and oral—he actually knew personally many of the men about whom he wrote. In a poem of such great length, however, the result is necessarily uneven. Thus, while some passages with valuable information are conveyed in a rather prosaic style, others in which the subject is frequently legendary, deserve praise for their poetic quality.

# EPILOGUE: *The New World and the World*

According to traditional knowledge established by Ptolemy, the world had three parts, Europe, Asia, and Africa. Renaissance Europe was still excited about the recovery of Greek and Roman texts when such a fundamental notion of geography was profoundly challenged. Naturally, it took Europeans a long time to accept and understand the full implications of having found what was to them a new part of the world. To be sure, Atlantic expeditions quickly uncovered the magnitude of that finding, and the increasing flow of goods and people across the Ocean Sea made the existence of America an established fact. Old notions proved resilient, however, and in spite of the growing literature about the New World, it seems that to many sixteenth-century European scholars America was no more than a minor appendix to the other three continents, and sometimes not even that much. As late as 1550, the German scholar Johannes Boemus published a book in Latin entitled "On the customs, laws, and rites of all peoples." It is not entirely surprising to find that no mention is made of the peoples of the New World. On the other hand, Spaniards were, for obvious reasons, less prone to such oversights. Thus, when a few years later Francisco Tamara, a professor at the University of Cadiz, edited a Spanish version of Boemus's work, he conveniently included a chapter of his own on the American Indians. This addition is reflected in the new title, *El libro de las costumbres de todas las gentes del mundo, y de las Indias* (No. 70). The juxtaposition of the world and the Indies, nevertheless, seems to suggest a still uncomfortable association between the two, rather than an integration of the Indies into the world.

By the seventeenth century things had changed, and such distinctions were no longer prevalent. Pedro Ordóñez de Cevallos (b. 1550?), a man with a formal education, travelled around the world for thirty-four years before his return to Madrid, where he became a priest. He then published an account of his observations entitled *Viaje del mundo* (No. 71). In the foreword, Ordóñez mentions having traveled more than thirty-thousand leagues across the five parts of the world: Europe, Africa, Asia, America, and "Megalamica." The latter is not Australia, still undiscovered, but actually Antarctica, at the time just a *terra incognita* south of the Magellan Straits. Ordóñez's account flows easily from one continent to another because of its autobiographical nature. A similar perspective is taken by Pedro Cubero Sebastián (1640–c. 1696), a priest who also recorded his missionary work around the world in a personal account of his travails entitled *Peregrinacion del mundo* (No. 72), and by Sebastián Fernández de Medrano (1646–1705), a scholar who never went to the New World. Medrano, director of the Military Academy of Brussels and the author of many books on military subjects, published in 1686 a *Breve descripcion del mundo* (No. 73). It was intended to be a useful book, a sort of geographic guide. It is interesting to note that Medrano, like

FIGURE 40. Pedro Cubero Sebastián. *Peregrinacion del mundo*. Naples, 1682. The female figures surrounding the globe represent the four continents—Europe wears a crown and the Pope's tiara is placed at her feet; Africa holds an ivory tusk; America, wearing her typical feather headdress, holds a bow and wears a quiver of arrows; Asia is represented with incense, precious stones, and spices at her feet.

Cubero, mentions America as one of the four parts of the world without any further explanation, therefore assuming that this is an accepted fact.

Beyond the scope of acceptance and description, the major role of historiography in the process of integrating America into the world was that of establishing the historical links between the Old and the New World. It was a formidable challenge to explain the origin of the Amerindian without questioning the basic tenets of the Biblical explanation of a single creation of man. Spanish historiographers showed no lack of imagination in dealing with that question, as Gregorio García's *Origen de los Indios* (No. 74) testifies. García (d. 1627), a Dominican who worked many years as a missionary in Mexico and Peru, wrote a comprehensive survey of all the theories that had been formulated to explain "the origin and cause of the Indians who inhabit these Western Indies, the newly-discovered fourth part of the world which present-day cosmographers call America." These included Acosta's theory of an early migration from Asia (No. 44), as well as others that postulated the existence of sailings by the lost twelve tribes of Israel, the Carthaginians, the Greeks, the Tartars, the Chinese, and so on. García's eclectic position on the issue favored a multiple migration, for he thought that a single origin would fail to explain the rich diversity of cultures found by the Europeans at the time of the Encounter.

García's work neatly exemplifies both the progress and the shortcomings of the long process, started in 1492, of assimilation of the Indies into the Old World. First seen as the offshore islands of Japan and China or the remnants of lost paradises, the New World had slowly taken shape as distinct continents with a particular history. As the confusion of 1492 faded away, America, no longer "new," became in the eyes of historians a familiar and equal player in the drama of world history.

# RELATED SECONDARY SOURCES

ADORNO, Rolena. *Guamán Poma. Writing and Resistance in Colonial Peru.* Austin: University of Texas Press, 1986.

—— and Walter MIGNOLO, eds. *Colonial Discourse.* Vol. XIV of *Dispositio* 36–38 (1989).

AMOR Y VÁZQUEZ, Jose. Intro. to Gabriel Lobo Lasso de la Vega, *Mexicana.* Madrid: Atlas, 1970, xiii–lviii.

AROCENA, Luis A. *Antonio de Solís, Cronista Indiano. Estudio sobre las formas historiográficas del Barroco.* Buenos Aires, EUDEBA, 1963.

—— *El inca Garcilaso y el humanismo de América.* Buenos Aires, 1949.

BLOCH, Ernst. *Historiography.* Chicago: Chicago Univ. Press, 1980.

CARBIA, Rómulo. *La crónica oficial de las Indias Occidentales.* Buenos Aires: Ediciones Buenos Aires, 1940.

ELLIOTT, J. H. "The Discovery of America and the Discovery of Man," in *Spain and Its World, 1500–1700.* New Haven: Yale Univ. Press, 1989, 42–64.

—— *The Old World and the New. 1492–1650.* Cambridge: Cambridge University Press, 1970.

ESTEVE BARBA, Francisco. *Historiografía indiana.* Madrid: Gredos, 1964.

FLORES, Angel. *The Literature of Spanish America, I. The Colonial Period.* New York: Las Americas Publishing Co., 1966.

FRIEDE, Juan. "La censura española del siglo XVI y los libros de historia de América." *Revista de historia de América* 47 (June, 1959), 45–94.

FUETER, Edmund. *Geschichte der neueren Historiographie.* Munich, 1911.

GERBI, Antonello. *Nature in the New World. From Christopher Columbus to Gonzalo Fernández de Oviedo.* Transl. Jeremy Moyle. Pittsburg: Univ. of Pittsburg Press, 1985.

GONZÁLEZ-ECHEVERRÍA, Roberto. "Humanismo, retórica y las crónicas de la conquista," in R. González-Echeverría, ed., *Historia y ficción en la narrativa hispanoamericana.* Caracas: Monte Avila, 1985.

—— "The Law of the Letter: Garcilaso's Commentaries and the Origins of Latin American Narrative." *The Yale Journal of Criticism* 1.1 (1987), 107–131.

HAY, Denis. *Annalists and Historians: Western Historiography from the VIIth to the XVIIth Century.* London: Methuen, 1977.

HOGDEN, Margaret. *Early Anthropology in the Sixteenth and Seventeenth Centuries.* Philadelphia: University of Pennsylvania Press, 1964.

JARA, René and Nicholas SPADACCINI, eds. *1492–1992: Re/Discovering Colonial Writing.* Vol. IV of *Hispanic Issues.* Minneapolis: The Prisma Institute, 1989.

LEÓN PORTILLA, Miguel, ed. *Visión de los vencidos. Relaciones indígenas de la conquista.* México: UNAM, 1959.

MADRIGAL, Luis Iñigo, ed. *Historia de la Literatura Hispanoamericana.* Vol. 1, Epoca colonial. Madrid: Cátedra, 1982.

MEDINA, José Toribio. *Bibliografía Hispanoamericana (1493–1810).* 7 vols. Santiago de Chile, 1898–1907.

MERRIM, Stephanie. "*Un mare magno e oculto:* Anatomy of Fenández de Oviedo's *Historia general y natural de las Indias.*" *Revista de Estudios Hispánicos* (1984), 101–120.

MIGNOLO, Walter. "El metatexto historiográfico y la historiografía indiana." *Modern Language Notes* 96 (1981), 358–402.

NORRIS, Y. E. "Estudios críticos sobre la historiografía latinoamericana," *Revista de Historia* 61–62 (1966), 245–312.

O'GORMAN, Edmundo. *The Invention of America.* Bloomington: Indiana Univ. Press, 1961.

—— *Cuatro historiadores de Indias. Siglo XVI. Pedro Mártir de Anglería, Gonzalo Fernández de Oviedo y Valdés, Fray Bartolomé de las Casas y Joseph de Acosta.* 2nd. ed. Mexico: Sep Diana, 1979.

PAGDEN, Anthony. *The Fall of Natural Man: the American Indian and the Origins of American Ethnology.* Cambridge: Cambridge University Press, 1982.

PASTOR, Beatriz. *Discursos narrativos de la conquista de América.* Hanover, NH: Ediciones del Norte, 1988.

PÉREZ, Joseph, ed. *La imagen del indio en la Europa moderna.* Madrid: Consejo Superior de Investigaciones Científicas, 1990.

PÉREZ DE TUDELA BUESO, Juan. *Significado histórico de la vida y escritos del Padre Las Casas.* Madrid: Biblioteca de Autores Españoles, 1958.

PUPO-WALKER, Enrique. *Historia, creación y profecía en los textos del Inca Garcilaso.* Madrid: José Porrúa, 1982.

—— *La vocación literaria del pensamiento histórico en América. Desarrollo de la prosa de ficción: Siglos xvi, xvii, xviii y xix.* Madrid: Gredos, 1982.

SALAS, Alberto M. *Tres cronistas de Indias. Pedro Mártir de Anglería. Gonzalo Fernández de Oviedo y Valdés. Fray Bartolomé de las Casas.* Mexico: Fondo de Cultura Económica, 1959.

SÁNCHEZ ALONSO, Benito. *Historia de la historiografía española.* 3 vols. Madrid: Consejo Superior de Investigaciones Científicas, 1947.

—— *Fuentes de la Historia Española e Hispanoamericana.* 3 vols. Madrid: Consejo Superior de Investigaciones Científicas, 1952.

TODOROV, Tzvetan. *The Conquest of America: The Question of the Other.* Trans. Richard Howard. New York: Harper and Row, 1984.

WILGUS, A. Curtis. *The Historiography of Latin America: A Guide to Historical Writing, 1500–1800.* Metuchen, N.J.: The Scarecrow Press, 1975.

—— *Histories and Historians of Hispanic America.* New York: Cooper Square Publishers, 1965.

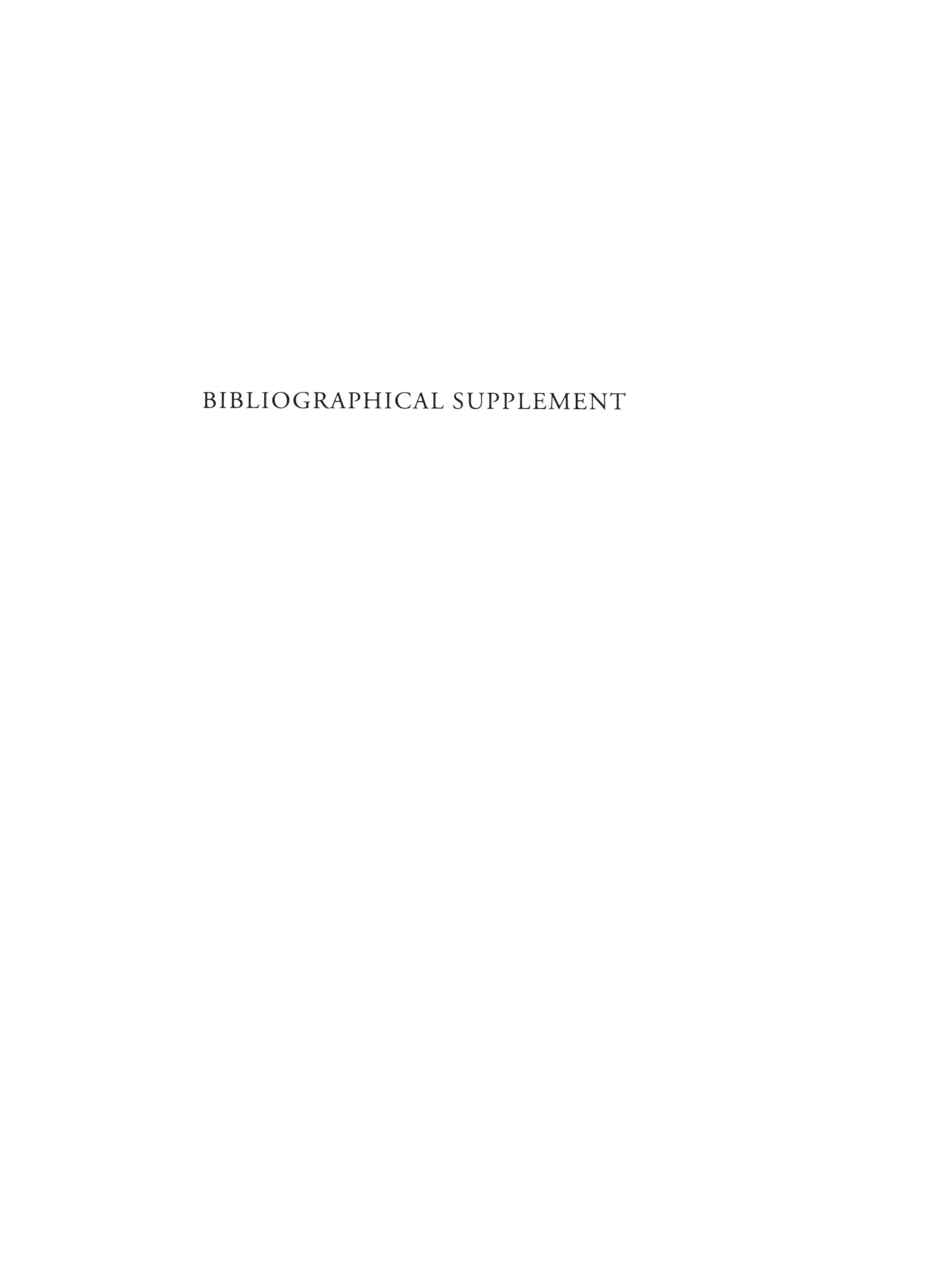

# BIBLIOGRAPHICAL SUPPLEMENT

# PREFACE

THIS Bibliographical Supplement has two parts. The first, headed "Bibliographical Descriptions," provides a full description of the earliest contemporary edition in the holdings of the John Carter Brown Library of each item featured in the exhibition catalogue. The second part of the Supplement, headed "Editions and Translations," is a short-title list of the many pre-1801 editions and translations of the featured primary works in the exhibition catalogue which may be found in the John Carter Brown Library collection. Works which were not printed until the nineteenth or twentieth centuries are excluded from this supplement as well as Number 11 which is not a part of the Library's collection. Much of the information presented here has also been entered into the international data base known as RLIN (Research Libraries Information Network).

With regard to the "Bibliographical Descriptions," the items are arranged alphabetically by author or, in the case of anonymous works, by title. A reference number preceding each work links it to the exhibition catalogue itself. The form of the author's name is governed by the *Anglo-American Cataloguing Rules*. Titles and imprints are literal transcriptions of spelling and punctuation, but capitalization is based on cataloguing rules. Typographical abbreviations have been expanded with the usage of brackets for the supplied parts. Omitted words are indicated by the customary three dots of elision. Imprint information which is taken from the colophon of a book is noted. A date of imprint which appears in Roman numerals is followed by the Arabic date in square brackets. Information which has been supplied from a secondary source is bracketed and justified in a note.

The collation line begins with the height of the book in centimeters followed by the format statement and signature collation, which includes, in parentheses, the location of blanks. The paginary collation is given in either pages or leaves as the case may be, bracketed if unnumbered. Errors in numbering are accounted for either in the collation itself or in a note. At the end of the paginary collation, plates and other illustrations are indicated.

Each description includes abbreviated references to published bibliographies which cite the book in question. A complete list of the references given in shortened form can be found at the beginning of the supplement. Copy-specific information about the Library's own holding, such as date of acquisition, imperfections in condition, and the presence of a contemporary binding, is also included. Location symbols for copies in the United States and Canada are provided at the end of each description, and a key to the symbols can also be found at the beginning of the supplement. These symbols represent libraries and institutions which have contributed cards to the *National Union Catalog, Pre-1956 Imprints*.

SUSAN L. NEWBURY
*Chief of Cataloguing*

# REFERENCES

Alden, *European Americana*
  *European Americana: a chronological guide to works printed in Europe relating to the Americas, 1493–1776.* Ed. by John Alden with the assistance of Dennis C. Landis. New York: Readex Books, 1980–

Backer-Sommervogel
  Backer, Augustine de. *Bibliothèque de la Compagnie de Jésus.* Nouv. éd. par Carlos Sommervogel. Brussels: O. Schepens; Paris: A. Picard, 1890–1932.
  ——— *Corrections & additions.* Par Ernest-M. Rivière. Toulouse: Rivière, 1911–1930.

Church, *Discovery*
  Church, Elihu Dwight. *A catalogue of books relating to the discovery and early history of North and South America forming a part of the library of E. D. Church.* Comp. and annotated by George Watson Cole. New York: Dood, Mead & Co.; Cambridge: University Press, 1907.

Fúrlong Cárdiff, *Antonio Ruiz de Montoya*
  Fúrlong Cárdiff, Guillermo. *Antonio Ruiz de Montoya y su carta a Comental, 1645.* Buenos Aires: Ediciones Theoría, 1964.

Goff
  Goff, Frederick Richmond. *Incunabula in American libraries; a third census of fifteenth-century books recorded in North American collections.* New York: Bibliographical Society of America, 1964. (Repr., Millwood, N.Y.: Kraus Reprint Co., 1973.)

Guerra, *Monardes*
  Guerra, Francisco. *Nicolás Bautista Monardes: su vida y su obra, c. 1493–1588.* Mexico, D.F.: Compañía Fundidora de Fierro y Acero de Monterrey, 1961.

GW
  *Gesamtkatalog der Wiegendrucke.* Leipzig: K. W. Hiersemann, 1925–1938. (Repr., New York: H. P. Kraus, 1968– )

J. C. Brown, Cat., 1493–1800
  Brown, John Carter. *Bibliotheca Americana: a catalogue of books relating to North and South America in the library of John Carter Brown of Providence, R.I.* Providence: Printed by H. O. Houghton & Co., Cambridge, 1865–1871.

J. C. Brown, Cat., 1482–1700
  Brown, John Carter. *Bibliotheca Americana: a catalogue of books relating to North and South America in the library of the late John Carter Brown of Providence, R.I.* Providence: Printed by H. O. Houghton & Co., Cambridge, 1875–1882.

JCB Lib. Cat., Pre-1675
  Brown University. John Carter Brown Library. *Bibliotheca Americana: catalogue of the John Carter Brown Library in Brown University, Providence, Rhode Island.* Providence: The Library, 1919–1931.

Medina, *Bib. hispano-americana*
  Medina, José Toribio. *Biblioteca hispano-americana (1493–1810).* Santiago [Chile], 1898–1907. (Repr., Santiago [Chile], 1958–1962.)

Medina, *Bib. hispano-chilena*
  Medina, José Toribio. *Biblioteca hispano-chilena (1523-1817).* Santiago [Chile]: The author, 1897–1899. (Repr., Amsterdam: N. Israel, 1965.)

Medina, *Lima*
  Medina, José Toribio. *La imprenta en Lima (1584–1824).* Santiago [Chile]: The author, 1904–1907. (Repr., Amsterdam: N. Israel, 1965.)

Medina, *México*
  Medina, José Toribio. *La imprenta en México (1539–1821).* Santiago [Chile]: The author, 1907–1912. (Repr., Amsterdam: N. Israel, 1965.)

Palau y Dulcet (2nd ed.)
  Palau y Dulcet, Antonio. *Manual del librero hispano-americano; bibliografía general española e hispano-americana desde la invención de la imprenta hasta nuestros tiempos, con el valor comercial de los impresos descritos.* 2. ed. corr. y aumentada por el autor. Barcelona: A. Palau, 1948–1977.

Peeters-Fontainas, *Bib. des impressions espagnoles*
  Peeters-Fontainas, Jean. *Bibliographie des impres-

*sions espagnoles des Pays-Bas méridionaux.* Louvain: J. Peeters-Fontainas, 1933. (Repr., Nieuwkoop: B. De Graaf, 1965.)

RETANA, *Aparato bib. de la historia general de Filipinas*
Retana y Gamboa, Wenceslao Emilio. *Aparato bibliográfico de la historia general de Filipinas deducido de la colección que posee en Barcelona la Compañia general de tabacos de dichas islas.* Madrid: Imprenta de la sucesora de M. Minuesa de los Ríos, 1906.

SABIN
Sabin, Joseph. *Bibliotheca Americana; a dictionary of books relating to America from its discovery to the present time.* Begun by Joseph Sabin, continued by Wilberforce Eames and completed by R.W.G. Vail, for the Bibliographical Society of America. New York: Sabin, 1868–1892; Bibliographical Society of America, 1928–1936. (Repr., Amsterdam: N. Israel, 1961–1962.)

STREIT, *Bib. missionum*
Streit, Robert. *Bibliotheca missionum.* Munich; Aachen, 1916–1966.

WAGNER, *Spanish Southwest*
Wagner, Henry Raup. *The Spanish Southwest, 1542–1794: an annotated bibliography.* Albuquerque: The Quivera Society, 1937.

# KEY TO LOCATION SYMBOLS

## California

| | |
|---|---|
| CCC | Honnold Library, Claremont Colleges. |
| CLCM | Los Angeles County Museum Library, Los Angeles. |
| CLSU | University of Southern California, Los Angeles. |
| CSmH | Henry E. Huntington Library, San Marino. |
| CU | University of California, Berkeley. |
| CU-A | University of California, Davis. |
| CU-B | University of California, Bancroft Library, Berkeley. |
| CU-S | University of California, San Diego, La Jolla. |

## Connecticut

| | |
|---|---|
| CtU | University of Connecticut, Storrs. |
| CtY | Yale University, New Haven. |

## District of Columbia

| | |
|---|---|
| DCU | Catholic University of America Library. |
| DDO | Dumbarton Oaks Research Library of Harvard University. |
| DFo | Folger Shakespeare Library. |
| DLC | U.S. Library of Congress. |
| DNLM | U.S. National Library of Medicine. |
| DPU | Pan American Union Library. |

## Florida

| | |
|---|---|
| FTaSU | Florida State University, Tallahassee. |

## Illinois

| | |
|---|---|
| ICJ | John Crerar Library, Chicago. |
| ICN | Newberry Library, Chicago. |
| IEN | Northwestern University, Evanston. |
| IMunS | Saint Mary of the Lake Seminary, Mundelein. |
| IU | University of Illinois, Urbana. |

## Indiana

| | |
|---|---|
| InU | Indiana University, Bloomington. |

## Iowa

| | |
|---|---|
| IaU | State University of Iowa, Iowa City. |

## Kansas

| | |
|---|---|
| KMK | Kansas State University, Manhattan. |

## Louisiana

| | |
|---|---|
| LNHT | Tulane University Library, New Orleans. |

## Maryland

| | |
|---|---|
| MdBP | Peabody Institute, Baltimore. |

## Massachusetts

| | |
|---|---|
| MB | Boston Public Library. |
| MBAt | Boston Athenaeum, Boston. |
| MH | Harvard University, Cambridge. |
| MH-A | Harvard University, Arnold Arboretum. |
| MH-P | Harvard University, Peabody Museum Library. |
| MU | University of Massachusetts, Amherst. |
| MWA | American Antiquarian Society, Worcester. |
| MWiW-C | Williams College, Williamstown, Chapin Library. |

## Michigan

| | |
|---|---|
| MiU | University of Michigan, Ann Arbor. |
| MiU-C | University of Michigan, William L. Clements Library. |

## Minnesota

| | |
|---|---|
| MnU | University of Minnesota, Minneapolis. |

## Missouri

| | |
|---|---|
| MoSU | St. Louis University, St. Louis. |
| MoSW | Washington University, St. Louis. |

## New Jersey

| | |
|---|---|
| NjP | Princeton University, Princeton. |
| NjR | Rutgers-The State University, New Brunswick. |

## New York

| | |
|---|---|
| NBC | Brooklyn College, Brooklyn. |
| NBuU | State University of New York at Buffalo. |
| NCH | Hamilton College, Clinton. |
| NHi | New York Historical Society, New York. |
| NIC | Cornell University, Ithaca. |
| NN | New York Public Library. |
| NNAHI | Augustinian Historical Institute, New York. |
| NNC | Columbia University, New York. |
| NNH | Hispanic Society of America, New York. |
| NNPM | Pierpont Morgan Library, New York. |
| NWM | U.S. Military Academy, West Point. |

## North Carolina

| | |
|---|---|
| NcD | Duke University, Durham. |
| NcU | University of North Carolina, Chapel Hill. |

## Ohio

| | |
|---|---|
| OC | Public Library of Cincinnati and Hamilton County, Cincinnati. |
| OCU | University of Cincinnati, Cincinnati. |
| OCl | Cleveland Public Library. |
| OClWHi | Western Reserve Historical Society, Cleveland. |
| OU | Ohio State University, Columbus. |

## Oregon

| | |
|---|---|
| OrU | University of Oregon, Eugene. |

## Pennsylvania

| | |
|---|---|
| PBL | Lehigh University, Bethlehem. |
| PBm | Bryn Mawr College, Bryn Mawr. |
| PHi | Historical Society of Pennsylvania, Philadelphia. |
| PP | Free Library of Philadelphia. |
| PPFr | Friends' Free Library of Germantown, Philadelphia. |
| PPL | Library Company of Philadelphia. |
| PPRF | Rosenbach Foundation, Philadelphia. |
| PPULC | Union Library Catalogue of Pennsylvania, Philadelphia. |
| PU | University of Pennsylvania, Philadelphia. |

## Rhode Island

| | |
|---|---|
| RPB | Brown University, Providence. |
| RPJCB | John Carter Brown Library, Providence. |

## South Carolina

| | |
|---|---|
| ScU | University of South Carolina, Columbia. |

## Texas

| | |
|---|---|
| TxU | University of Texas, Austin. |

## Utah

| | |
|---|---|
| UU | University of Utah, Salt Lake City. |

## Virginia

| | |
|---|---|
| ViU | University of Virginia, Charlottesville. |
| ViW | College of William and Mary, Williamsburg. |

## Washington

| | |
|---|---|
| WaU | University of Washington, Seattle. |

## Wisconsin

| | |
|---|---|
| WU | University of Wisconsin, Madison. |

## Canada

| | |
|---|---|
| CaBVaU | University of British Columbia Library, Vancouver. |
| CaBViPA | Provincial Archives, Victoria. |

# BIBLIOGRAPHICAL DESCRIPTIONS

## 44

ACOSTA, JOSÉ DE, 1540–1600.

Historia natural y moral delas Indias, en que se tratan las cosas notables del cielo, y elementos, metales . . . y guerras de los Indios. Compuesta por el padre Ioseph de Acosta religioso de la Compañia de Iesus. . . .

Impresso en Seuilla en casa de Iuan de Leon. Año de 1590.

COLLATION: 21 cm. (4to): A⁶ B–2K⁸ 2L⁶ 2M⁸ 2N¹⁰ (2N10 verso blank). 535, [37] p.

NOTES: Books 1–2 originally appeared in Latin as: De natura Novi Orbis libro duo, Salamanca, 1588. Title vignette: Jesuit trigram. Includes index.

REFERENCES: JCB Lib. cat., pre-1675, I, p. 321; Alden, *European Americana*, 590/1.

JCB LIBRARY COPY: Acquired in 1846. Lacks the leaf of errata and tax statement inserted between p. 4–5.

COPIES: DLC, MnU, ViU, PPULC, NjP, CCC. ScU, RPB, MiU-C, MH-A, PHi, PPL, ViW, MH, NNH, RPJCB, NWM, CU, MB, NN.

## 37

ACUÑA, CRISTÓBAL DE, b. 1597.

Nueuo descubrimiento del gran rio de las Amazonas. Por el padre Chrstoval [*sic*] de Acuña, religioso de la Compañia de Iesus, y calificador de la Suprema General Inquisicion. Al qual fue, y se hizo por orden de Su Magestad, el año de 1639. Por la prouincia de Quito en los reynos del Perù. . . .

En Madrid, en la Imprenta del Reyno, año de 1641.

COLLATION: 21 cm. (4to): ¶⁴ 2¶² A-L⁴ M². [6], 46 leaves.

NOTES: Title vignette: Jesuit trigram. An account of the expedition under Pedro Teixeira. "Memorial, presentado en el Real Consejo de las Indias, sobre el dicho descubrimiento, despues del reuelion de Portugal," leaves 43–46.

REFERENCES: JCB Lib. cat., pre-1675, II, p. 287; Alden, *European Americana*, 641/2; Medina, *Bib. hispano-americana*, 1022; Palau y Dulcet (2nd ed.), 2479.

JCB LIBRARY COPY: Acquired in 1846. Contains commentary in manuscript (3 p.) bound in at front.

COPIES: DLC, NN, RPJCB, CtY, LNHT, OC, NjP, MnU, MiU-C, MH, NNH, PBL.

## 25

ALBENINO, NICOLAO DE, b. 1514?

Verdadera relacion: de lo sussedido en los reynos e prouincias d[e]l Peru / de[s]de la yda a ellos d[e]l virey Blasco Nuñes Vela / hasta el desbarato y muerte de Gonçalo Piçarro.

Seuilla a dos dias del mes de enero del año de Christo de .M.D.xlix. en casa de Juan de Leon. [1549]

COLLATION: 17 cm. (8vo): a–k⁸. [160] p.

NOTES: Illustrated title page. Author's name appears on verso of title page. Dedicatory epistle on p. [3–5] signed: Fernan Xuares. Publication statement from colophon.

REFERENCES: Alden, *European Americana*, 549/1; Medina, *Bib. hispano-americana*, 137.

JCB LIBRARY COPY: Acquired in 1939.

COPIES: NN, LNHT, RPJCB.

## 3

ANGHIERA, PIETRO MARTIRE D', 1457–1526.

Ioannes Ruffus Foroliuiensis Archiep[iscop]us Co[n]sentin[us]: legat[us] apo. ad lectore[m] De orbe nouo. . . . De orbe nouo decades.

Impressæ in contubernio Arnaldi Guillelmi in illustri oppido Carpetanæ p[ro]ui[n]ciæ Co[m]pluto quod uulgariter dicitur Alcala p[er]fectu[m] est nonis Noue[m]bris An. 1516.

COLLATION: 31 cm. (fol.): a⁶ b–g⁸ h⁶ i⁸ A–B⁸ (i5, i8 verso, B8 verso blank). [84] leaves.

NOTES: The first three decades of Anghiera's: De orbe novo; edited by Antonio de Nebrija. The first nine books of decade 1 and a part of book 10 originally published as part of: P. Martyris Angli Mediolanensis Opera. Seville, 1511, under title: Occeani decas. In this edition, the part of book 10 of the first decade originally published in 1511 is added to the ninth book, and the text of book 10 as well as that of decades 2–3 is published for the first time. Another issue of the same year published under title: Argumenta trium decadum tibi lector habeto. . . . De orbe nouo decades et Legatio Babylonica. Alcala de Henares, 1516. Author's name given in headline on leaf [2] recto: P. Martyris Angli Mediolanensis. Publication statement from colophon on leaf [68] recto. Title surrounded by ornamental border. Errata statement on leaf [64]. Includes "Vocabula Barbara" (leaves [66–68] recto). "Legatio Babylonica" has separate signatures, but no special title page (leaves [69–84]) and is lacking in some copies. This section also originally published as part of: P. Martyris Angli Mediolanensis Opera. Seville, 1511.

REFERENCES: JCB Lib. cat., pre-1675, I, p. 66; Alden, *European Americana*, 516/1; Medina, *Bib. hispano-americana*, 53; Palau y Dulcet (2nd ed.), 12590.

JCB LIBRARY COPY: Acquired in 1846. This copy has portrait of author pasted to front flyleaf.

COPIES: DLC, CSmH, MWiW-C, NN, NjP, LNHT, RPJCB, InU, ICN, MiU-C, ViU, MnU.

## 68

BARCO CENTENERA, MARTÍN DEL, b. 1535.

Argentina y conquista del Rio de la Plata, con otros acaecimientos de los reynos del Peru, Tucuman, y estado del Brasil, por el arcediano don Martin del Barco Centenera. . . .

En Lisboa, por Pedro Crasbeeck. 1602.

COLLATION: 19 cm. (4to): π⁴ A-2E⁸ 2F⁶ (2F6 verso blank). [4], 230 leaves.

NOTES: In verse.

REFERENCES: JCB Lib. cat., pre-1675, II, p. 14; Alden, *European Americana*, 602/11; Medina, *Bib. hispano-americana*, 459.

JCB LIBRARY COPY: Acquired in 1846.

COPIES: MH, CtY, NBC, RPJCB.

## 54

CALANCHA, ANTONIO DE LA, 1584–1654.

Coronica moralizada del orden de San Augustin en el Peru, con sucesos egenplares en esta monarquia. Compuesta por el muy reverendo padre maestro fray Antonio de la Calancha de la misma orden, i difinidor actual. Dividese este primer tomo en quatro libros; lleva tablas de capitulos, i lugares de la Sagrada Escritura.

Año 1639. En Barcelona: por Pedro Lacavalleria, en la calle de la libreria.

COLLATION: 34 cm. (fol.): π1 *⁶ 2*⁸ A–3I⁶ 3L–4K⁶ 4L⁸ (4L8 verso blank). [30], 884, 883–922, [28] p., [1] folded leaf of plates; ill.

NOTES: This first volume originally published: Barcelona, 1638. Vol. 2, written in part by Bernardo de Torres, was printed at Lima in 1653; cf. Medina, *Lima*, 350. Added engraved title page reads: Chronica moralizada del orden de S. Augustin en el Peru, and is signed: Pet. de Iode Iunior sculpsit. Contains numerous errors in paging.

REFERENCES: JCB Lib. cat., pre-1675, II, p. 267; Alden, *European Americana*, 639/26.

JCB LIBRARY COPY: Acquired in 1851. This copy contains some foxing and worming with slight losses of text; the date on the title page has been cut out and replaced with the 1638 date.

COPIES: ICN, NcD, CtY, NN, MBAt, RPJCB, OCU.

## 43

CASAS, BARTOLOMÉ DE LAS, 1474–1556.

Breuissima relacion de la destruycion de las Indias: colegida por el obispo do[n] fray Bartolome de las Casas / o Casaus de la Orden de Sa[n]cto Domingo. Año. 1552.

Fue impressa . . . enla . . . ciudad de Seuilla en casa de Sebastian Trugillo . . . a Nuestra Señora de Gracia. Año de. M.D.Lij. [1552, i.e. not before 1553]

COLLATION: 20 cm. (4to): a–e⁸ f¹⁰ g⁴ ²a–²g⁸ h⁶ ³a¹⁰ ⁴a–³c⁸ ³d¹² ⁵a–³f⁸ ³g⁶ ⁶a¹⁶ ⁷a–k⁸ A¹⁰ (h6, ³g6 blank). 9 parts ([644] p.)

NOTES: Publication statement from colophon of first tract: leaf f10 recto. Seven of the titles are within ornamental borders; two of the tracts have caption titles only. Church indicates that these nine tracts, published by the author in defence of the Indians, constitute a collection for which bibliographers have determined no particular arrangement. The individual works were printed between 1552 and 1553 and the complete set could not have been issued before 1553. Contains: Breuissima relacion de la destruycion de las Indias . . . Seville : Sebastian Trugillo, 1552., [100] p.—Lo que se sigue es vn pedaço de vna carta . . . [Seville : Sebastian Trugillo, 1552], [8] p.—Aqui se contiene vna disputa / o controuersia . . . Seville : Sebastian Trugillo, 1552., [124] p.—Aqui se co[n]tiene[n] treynta proposiciones muy juridicas . . . Seville : Sebastian Trugillo, 1552., [20] p.—Esta es vn tratado . . . Seville : Sebastian Trugillo, 1552., [72] p.—Entre los remedios . . . Seville : Jacome Cromberger, 1552., [108] p.—Aqui se co[n]tiene[n] vnos auisos y reglas . . . Seville : Sebastian Trugillo, 1552., [32] p.—Tratado co[m]probatorio del Imperio soberano . . . Seville : Sebastian Trugillo, 1553., [160] p.—Principia queda[m] ex quibus procedendum est in disputatione . . . Seville : Sebastian Trugillo, [1552], [20] p.

REFERENCES: JCB Lib. cat., pre-1675, I, p. 167; Alden, *European Americana*, 552/8-15; Church, *Discovery*, 87–96.

JCB LIBRARY COPY: Acquired in 1846. Contains contemporary marginal manuscript notes with some partially lost due to trimming. The first gathering "a" is bound out of order. The eighth tract in this copy (Tratado co[m]probatorio) has printed cancel slips of two lines each, pasted at the bottom of the rectos of leaves [e5] and [f6]. This copy has three manuscript tracts bound in at the end: Resolucion, y declaracion, a 12 dudas por don fray Bartholome de las Casas; Singularis tractatus . . . D. F. Bartholomei a Casaus . . . super quoddam quaesitum ad novum Indiarum orbem attinens; Apologia Ioanis Genesii Sepulvedae pro libro De iustis belli causis.

COPIES: MH, MWiW-C, CtY, OCl, LNHT, ViU, RPJCB, CU-B, MB, MBAt, NN, CSmH, DLC, PPULC, NNH, MiU-C, PPRF, FTaSU.

## 69

CASTELLANOS, JUAN DE, 1522–1607.

Primera parte, de las elegias de varones illustres de Indias. Compuestas por Juan de Castellanos . . .

En Madrid, en casa de la viuda de Alonso Gomez impressor de Su Magestad. Año. 1589.

COLLATION: 21 cm. (4to): ¶⁴ A⁶ B–Z⁸ 2A⁸ (2A8 blank). [20], 64, 63–318, 337–382, [2] p.; ill., port.

NOTES: No more of the original edition published. In verse. Errata statement on p. [4].

REFERENCES: JCB Lib. cat., pre-1675, I, p. 315; Alden, *European Americana*, 589/15.

JCB LIBRARY COPY: Acquired in 1846. Lacks last leaf (blank). Pages 85–86 misbound before p. 83, and p. 87–88 misbound after p. 90.

COPIES: DLC, NNH, LNHT, NN, PBL, RPJCB.

## 26

CIEZA DE LEÓN, PEDRO DE, 1518–1554.

Parte primera dela chronica del Peru. Que tracta la demarcacion de sus prouincias: la descripcion dellas. Las fundaciones de las nueuas ciudades. Los ritos y costumbres de los indios. Y otras cosas estrañas dignas de ser sabidas. Fecha por Pedro d[e] Cieza de Leon vezino de Seuilla. 1553. . . .

Impressa en Seuilla en casa de Martin de Montesdoca. Acabose a quinze de março de mill y quinientos y cinquenta y tres años. [1553]

COLLATION: 29 cm. (fol.): +⁶–2+⁴ a–q⁸ r⁶. [10], cxxxiiij leaves; ill.

NOTES: Publication statement taken from colophon. Title vignette: royal arms. Errata statement on leaf [10] verso. The "Chronica" left by Cieza de Leon was divided into four parts; only the first part was published before the 19th century.

REFERENCES: JCB Lib. cat., pre-1675, I, p. 175; Alden, *European Americana*, 553/20; Medina, *Bib. hispano-americana*, 157; Palau y Dulcet (2nd ed.), 54646.

JCB LIBRARY COPY: Acquired before 1866. Part of the margin of the title page is wanting; restored in pen and ink facsimile.

COPIES: DLC, ICN, RPJCB, NNH, NN, ViU.

## 60

COLÓN, FERNANDO, 1488–1539.

Historie del S. D. Fernando Colombo; nelle quali s'ha particolare, & vera relatione della vita, & de'fatti dell'ammiraglio D. Christoforo Colombo, suo padre: et dello scoprimento, ch'egli fece dell'Indie Occidentali, dette Mondo Nuouo, hora possedute dal sereniss. re catolico: nuouamente di lingua spagnuola tradotte nell'italiana dal S. Alfonso Vlloa. . . .

In Venetia, M D LXXI. Appresso Francesco de'Franceschi Sanese. [1571]

COLLATION: 15 cm. (8vo): a–b⁸ c⁴ A–2G⁸ 2H⁸ (–2H8) (c4 blank). [20], 247 leaves.

NOTES: Title vignette: printer's device. Errata statement on leaf [19] verso. The 'Venice 1569' copy at Princeton (as noted in the Library of Congress Catalog) is reported by the Curator of Rare Books to be an altered copy, probably of the Venice 1709 edition. Includes index. "Scrittura di fra Roman [i.e. Ramón Pane] delle antichitá de gl'Indiani . . . ," leaves 126 verso–145 verso. "Whether or not this is, as represented, from Columbus's son's pen has, in the absence of the Spanish original, long been a matter of dispute"; cf. Alden.

REFERENCES: JCB Lib. cat., pre-1675, I, p. 244; Alden, *European Americana*, 571/8.

JCB LIBRARY COPY: Acquired in 1846. Leaf 124 is misbound before leaf 123, and leaf 126 is misbound before leaf 125.

COPIES: CSmH, MiU-C, NcU, MB, DLC, NNH, MBAt, MnU, MWiW-C, ViW, NjP, CtY, RPJCB.

I

COLUMBUS, CHRISTOPHER.

Epistola Christofori Colom: cui [a]etas nostra multu[m] debet: de insulis Indi[a]e supra Gangem nuper inuentis. Ad quas perquirendas octauo antea mense auspicijs [et] [a]ere inuictissimi Fernandi Hispaniarum Regis missus fuerat: as magnificum d[omi]n[u]m Raphaelem Sanxis . . . missa: quam . . . Aliander de Cosco ab Hispano ideomate in latinum conuertit: tertio kal[enda]s Maij M.cccc.xciij. Pontificatus Alexandri Sexti anno primo.

[Rome : S. Plannck, after 29 Apr. 1493]

COLLATION: 20 cm. (4to): [8] p.

NOTES: Translation of: Senor por que se que aureis plazer de la grand vitoria, Barcelona, 1493, and generally considered to be the first Latin edition. Caption title. Publication statement from *Gesamtkatalog der Wiegendrucke*. Leaves unsigned. Has 34 lines to a full page.

REFERENCES: JCB Lib. cat., pre-1675, I, p. 17; GW, 7173; Goff, C–757; Alden, *European Americana*, 493/4.

JCB LIBRARY COPY: Acquired in 1887.

COPIES: ICN, InU, MB, NN, RPJCB, NNPM, MiU-C, CLSU.

57

CÓRDOVA SALINAS, DIEGO DE.

Vida, virtudes, y milagros del apostol del Peru el B. P. Fr. Francisco Solano, de la serafica orden de los menores de la regular obseruancia, patron de la ciudad de Lima. Sacada de las declaraciones de quinientos testigos . . . Por el P. Fr. Diego de Cordoua . . . del orden de N. P. S. Francisco. Tercera impression, que saca a luz el M. R. P. Fr. Pedro de Mena . . .

En Madrid: en la Imprenta Real. Año de 1676.

COLLATION: 21 cm. (4to): §⁸ 2§² A–2L⁸ 2M⁴. [20], 544, [8] p.

NOTES: Originally published: Lima, 1630.

REFERENCES: Sabin, 86229; Medina, *Bib. hispano-americana*, 1608; Streit, *Bib. missionum*, II:2111.

JCB LIBRARY COPY: Acquired in 1978. Bound in contemporary vellum.

COPIES: CtY, ICN, RPJCB.

7a

CORTÉS, HERNÁN, 1485–1547.

Carta de relacio[n] e[m]biada a Su. S. Majestad del e[m]p[er]ador n[uest]ro señor por el capita[n] general dela Nueua Spaña: llamado Ferna[n]do Cortes. Enla q[ua]l haze relacio[n] d[e]las tierras y proui[n]cias sin cue[n]to q[ue] ha[n] descubierto nueuame[n]te enel Yucata[n] del año de .xix. a esta p[ar]te: y ha sometido ala corona real de Su S. M. . . .

Fue impressa enla muy noble [et] muy leal ciudad de Seuilla: por Jacobo Cro[m]berger aleman. A .viij. dias nouie[m]bre. Año de M.d. [et] xxij. [1522]

COLLATION: 31 cm. (fol.): a–c⁸ d⁴. [56] p.

NOTES: Cortés's second letter to Charles V. Publication statement from colophon. Illustrated title page: portrait of the Emperor.

REFERENCES: JCB Lib. cat., pre-1675, I, p. 81; Alden, *European Americana*, 522/5; Medina, *Bib. hispano-americana*, 64.

JCB LIBRARY COPY: Acquired in 1847.

COPIES: CSmH, NN, RPJCB.

## 7B

CORTÉS, HERNÁN, 1485–1547.

Carta tercera de relacio[n]: embiada por Ferna[n]do Cortes capitan [y] justicia mayor del Yucatan llamado la Nueua España del mar oceano: al muy alto y potentissimo cesar [y] i[n]uictissimo señor do[n] Carlos emperador semper augusto y rey de España nuestro señor: delas cosas sucedidas [y] muy dignas de admiracion enla conquista y recuperacion dela muy grande [y] marauillosa ciudad de Temixtitan: y delas otras prouincias a ella subjetas que se rebelaron. Enla qual ciudad [y] dichas prouincias el dicho capitan y españoles consiguieron grandes y señaladas victorias dignas de perpetua memoria. Assi mesmo haze relacion como ha[n] descubierto el mar del Sur: [y] otras muchas [y] gra[n]des prouincias muy ricas de minas de oro: y perlas: y piedras preciosas: [y] avn tienen noticia que ay especeria.

Fue impressa e[n]la ... ciudad d[e] Seuilla por Jacobo Cro[m]berger alema[n]: acabose a .xxx. dias de março: año d[e] mill [y] quinie[n]tos [y] xxiij. [1523]

COLLATION: 29 cm. (fol.): a–c⁸ d⁶ (d6 verso blank). [60] p.

NOTES: Publication statement from colophon. Illustrated title page: portrait of the Emperor.

REFERENCES: JCB Lib. cat., pre-1675, I, p. 86; Alden, *European Americana*, 523/4; Medina, *Bib. hispano-americana*, 66.

JCB LIBRARY COPIES: Copy 1 acquired in 1851. This copy bound with his: Carta de relacion. Saragossa, 1523. Copy 2 acquired in 1846. This copy bound separately.

COPIES: NN, ICN, NNH, RPJCB, CSmH.

## 7C

CORTÉS, HERNÁN, 1485–1547.

La quarta relacion q[ue] Ferna[n]do Cortes gouernador y capitan general por Su Majestad enla Nueua España d[e]l mar oceano embio al muy alto [y] muy potentissimo inuictissimo señor don Carlos emperador semper angusto [*sic*] y rey de España nuestro señor: enla qual estan otras cartas [y] relaciones que los capitanes Pedro de Aluarado [y] Diego Godoy embiaron al dicho capitan Fernardo [*sic*] Cortes.

Fue impressa ... en ... Toledo por Gaspar de Auila. Acabose a veynte dias del mes de octubre. Año del nascimiento de Nuestro Saluador Jesu Christo de mil [y] quinientos [y] veynte y cinco años. [1525]

COLLATION: 29 cm. (fol.): a⁶ b–c⁸ (c8 blank). [44] p.

NOTES: Publication statement from colophon. Illustrated title page: coat of arms of Spain.

REFERENCES: JCB Lib. cat., pre-1675, I, p. 94; Alden, *European Americana*, 525/4; Medina, *Bib. hispano-americana*, 73.

JCB LIBRARY COPY: Acquired in 1851. This copy bound with his: Carta de relacion. Saragossa, 1523. Lacks last leaf (blank).

COPIES: CSmH, NN, RPJCB.

## 72

CUBERO SEBASTIÁN, PEDRO, 1640–c. 1696.

Peregrinacion del mundo, del doctor D. Pedro Cubero Sebastian, predicador apostolico....

En Napoles, por Carlos Porsile 1682.

COLLATION: 21 cm. (4to): a⁶ A–3L⁴. [12], 451, [5] p., [3] leaves of plates; ports.

NOTES: Added engraved half title with inscription: Ad istanza del Sr. Gioseppe Criscolo A. 1682. Preliminary matter includes poetry by Pedro Calderon de la Barca, Juan de Matos Fragoso, and Antonio de Cardenas. Originally published as: Breve relación de la peregrinación, Madrid, 1680.

REFERENCES: Palau y Dulcet (2nd ed.), 65757; Medina, *Bib. hispano-americana*, 1728; Streit, *Bib. missionum*, V:555.

JCB LIBRARY COPY: Acquired in 1915.

COPIES: NN, TxU, RPJCB.

## 49

DÁVILA PADILLA, AGUSTÍN, 1562–1604.

Historia de la fundacion y discurso de la prouincia de Santiago de Mexico, de la Orden de Predicadores, por las vidas de sus varones insignes, y casos notables de

Nueua España. Por el maestro fray Augustin Dauila Padilla. . . .

En Madrid en casa de Pedro Madrigal. Año de 1596.

COLLATION: 30 cm. (fol.): ¶⁶ A–2X⁶ 2Z–3Z⁶ 4A⁸ (¶3, 3Y6, and 4A8 versos blank). [12], 280, 291–686, 689–815, [29] p.; ill.

NOTES: Errata statements on leaves ¶2 recto and ¶6 verso. Includes index.

REFERENCES: JCB Lib. cat., pre-1675, I, p. 341; Alden, *European Americana*, 596/32.

JCB LIBRARY COPY: Acquired in 1847. Has p. 305–306 misbound before p. 303–304; p. 365–366 misbound before p. 363–364; p. 677–678 misbound before p. 675–676; and p. 703–704 misbound before p. 701–702.

COPIES: DLC, RPJCB.

10

DÍAZ DEL CASTILLO, BERNAL, 1496–1584.

Historia verdadera de la conquista de la Nueua España. Escrita por el capitan Bernal Diaz del Castillo, vno de sus conquistadores. Sacada a luz, por el P. M. Fr. Alonso Remon, predicador y coronista general del Orden de N. S. de la Merced, redencion de cautiuos.

En Madrid, en la emprenta del reyno [1632]

COLLATION: 28 cm. (fol.): ¶⁴ *⁶ A–2H⁸ 2I⁶ 2K². [10], 256 leaves, [1] leaf of plates.

NOTES: Originally published earlier the same year with 211 chapters; this later edition has one additional chapter (misnumbered CCXXII). Engraved title page signed: I. de Courbes F. Date of publication based on Alden. Two states noted: in one state leaf 68 misnumbered 67; in the other state this leaf is correctly numbered. Numerous errors in paging.

REFERENCES: J. C. Brown, Cat., 1482–1700, II:387; Alden, *European Americana*, 632/28; Medina, *Bib. hispano-americana*, 899.

JCB LIBRARY COPIES: Copy 1 acquired in 1940. This copy is bound in contemporary vellum, has leaf 68 misnumbered 67, lacks leaves 254–255, and has leaves 253 and 256 repaired with slight losses of text. Copy 2 acquired in 1846. This copy has leaf 68 correctly numbered, and gathering * (Tabla de los capitulos) is misbound at end.

COPIES: RPJCB, DLC, NNH, NjP, PPL, NN, LNHT, PBm, CtY, InU.

5

ENCISO, MARTÍN FERNÁNDEZ DE.

Suma de geographia q[ue] trata de todas las partidas [y] prouincias del mundo: en especial de las Indias. [Y] trata largeme[n]te del arte del marear: junctame[n]te con la espera en roma[n]ce: con el regimie[n]to del sol [y] del norte: nueuamente hecha. . . .

Fue impressa en la . . . ciudad de Seuilla por Jacobo Cro[m]berger alema[n] en el año d[e]la encarnacion de Nuestro Señor. de mil [y] quinientos [y] diez [y] nueue. [1519]

COLLATION: 30 cm. (fol.): a–b¹⁴ c–h⁸ (h8 blank). [152] p.; ill.

NOTES: Publication statement from colophon. Illustrated title page. Dedication (p. [3]) by Martin Ferna[n]dez Denciso.

REFERENCES: JCB Lib. cat., pre-1675, I, p. 73; Alden, *European Americana*, 519/4; Medina, *Bib. hispano-americana*, 56.

JCB LIBRARY COPY: Acquired in 1848. Lacks leaf h8 (blank).

COPIES: DLC, NNH, CSmH, CU-B, MnU, MiU-C, NN, RPJCB, MH, InU.

62

ERCILLA Y ZÚÑIGA, ALONSO DE, 1533–1594.

La Araucana de don Alonso de Ercilla y Çuñiga. . . .

En Salamanca, en casa de Domingo de Portonarijs . . . 1574 . . . A costa de Vicente, y Simon de Portonarijs.

COLLATION: 14 cm. (8vo): †⁸ 2†⁴ A–2B⁸. [24], 392, [8] p.; port.

NOTES: Narrative poem on Spanish efforts to subdue Araucanian Indians. Title vignette. This part originally published: Madrid, 1569. Includes index.

REFERENCES: Alden, *European Americana*, 574/17; Medina, *Bib. hispano-americana*, 233.

JCB LIBRARY COPY: Acquired in 1962. Bound in contemporary vellum. Has title page and p. 197–198 damaged with some loss of text.

COPIES: NNH, RPJCB.

## 28

FERNÁNDEZ, DIEGO, c. 1520–c. 1581.

Primera, y segunda parte, de la historia del Peru, que se mando escreuir, à Diego Fernandez... Co[n]tiene la primera, lo succedido en la Nueua España y en el Perù, sobre la execucion de las nueuas leyes: y el allanamiento, y castigo, que hizo el presidente Gasca, de Gonçalo Piçarro y sus sequaces. La segunda, contiene, la tyrannia y alçamiento de los contreras, y don Sebastia[n] de Castilla, y de Francisco Herna[n]dez Giron: con otros muchos acaescimientos y successos....
Fue impresso en Seuilla en casa de Hernando Diaz en la calle de la sierpe. Año de 1571.

COLLATION: 28 cm. (fol.): A⁴ B–R⁸ S¹⁰ *⁴ 2A–2P⁸ 2Q⁶ (2Q6 verso blank). [4], 130, 135–142, 130 leaves.

NOTES: Illustrated title pages. In addition to the general title page, each part has a special title page: "La primera parte de la historia del Peru" and "La segunda parte de la historia del Peru"; the special title page for part 1 is not present in all copies. Also, each part has separate foliation and signatures.

REFERENCES: JCB Lib. cat., pre-1675, I, p. 244; Alden, *European Americana*, 571/10.

JCB LIBRARY COPY: Acquired in 1846. Lacks the special title page to part 1; available in facsimile. Has author's signature at end of part 2.

COPIES: MWiW-C, MB, NN, RPB, RPJCB, DLC, PU, NHi, NBuU, MiU-C, NcD, CtY, ICN, NNH.

## 73

FERNÁNDEZ DE MEDRANO, SEBASTIÁN, 1646–1705.

Breve descripcion del mundo, y sus partes, ò guia geographica, y hydrographica, dividida en tres libros.... Por el capitan D. Sebastian Fernandez de Medrano, maestro de mathematicas de la Academia militar del exercito de los estados de Flandes.
En Brusselas, en casa de los herederos de Francisco Foppens. 1686.

COLLATION: 16 cm. (8vo): *⁸ 2*⁸ (–2*8) A–2C⁸ (2C8 blank). [30], 64, 63–412, [2] p., [5] folded leaves of plates; ill., maps.

REFERENCES: Sabin, 47358; Medina, *Bib. hispano-americana*, 1787; Palau y Dulcet (2nd ed.), 89225.

JCB LIBRARY COPY: Acquired in 1974.

COPIES: CtY, NN, UU, RPJCB.

## 6

FERNÁNDEZ DE OVIEDO Y VALDÉS, GONZALO, 1478–1557.

Ouiedo Dela natural hystoria delas Indias....
Se imprimio a costas del autor Go[n]çalo Ferna[n]dez de Ouiedo al[ia]s de Valdes. Por industria de maestre Remo[n] de Petras: [et] se acabo en la cibdad de Toledo a. xv. dias del mes de hebrero. de .M.D. xxvj. años. [1526]

COLLATION: 31 cm. (fol.): A–C⁸ D–H⁶. lij, [2] leaves; ill.

NOTES: Verso of title page: Sumario dela natural y general istoria delas Indias. Que escriuio Go[n]çalo Ferna[n]dez de Ouiedo alias de Valdes. This work is not a summary of the author's later work: La historia general de las Indias, Seville, 1535, but quite an independent account. Publication statement from colophon. Includes index. Illustrated title page, with coat of arms of Charles V in center and a medallion, for author's autograph signature, at bottom. Leaf xl misnumbered xlj.

REFERENCES: JCB Lib. cat., pre-1675, I, p. 96, Alden, *European Americana*, 526/5; Medina, *Bib. hispano-americana*, 75; Palau y Dulcet (2nd ed.), 89527.

JCB LIBRARY COPY: Acquired before 1853. Has author's signature in medallion on title page.

COPIES: DLC, CU, NjP, NN, ViU, NNH, RPJCB, MiU-C, InU.

## 41

FERNÁNDEZ DE OVIEDO Y VALDÉS, GONZALO, 1478–1557.

La historia general delas Indias.
Sevilla / enla empre[n]ta de Juam Cromberger / el postrero dia del mes de setiembre. Año de mil y quinientos y treynta y cinco años. [1535]

COLLATION: 30 cm. (fol.): +⁴ a–z⁸ &¹⁰ (&10 blank). [4], cxciij, [1] leaves; ill., coat of arms.

NOTES: A distinct work from the author's 1526: De la natural hystoria de las Indias. Containing 19 books and a few chapters of book 50, this work is complete in itself, although Oviedo left a much longer manuscript. Book 20 was printed in 1557, but the entire work of 50 books wasn't printed until 1851–1855. Publication statement from colophon on leaf cxcj verso. Leaf lxxvij misnumbered lxxvj. Title vignette: arms of Charles V. Coat of arms of author on verso of leaf cxciij. Verso of title leaf: Primera parte de la historia natural y general delas indias. Leaves cxcij–cxciij: Epistola. Siguese una carta missiva con que el cronista y auctor destas historias embio este volumen y primera parte dellas / assi como se acabaron de imprimir. Al . . . don fray Garcia Jofre de Loaysa . . . (to which the author has attached his signature).

REFERENCES: JCB Lib. cat., pre-1675, I, p. 118; Alden, *European Americana*, 535/12; Medina, *Bib. hispano-americana*, 97.

JCB LIBRARY COPY: Acquired in 1846. Lacks last leaf (blank).

COPIES: RPJCB, DLC, InU, MnU, MB, NN, NNH, MiU-C, MWiW-C.

## 35

FERNÁNDEZ DE PIEDRAHITA, LUCAS, 1624–1688.

Historia general de las conquistas del nuevo reyno de Granada.

Amberes. Por Juan Baptista Verdussen. [i.e. Seville, Tomás de Haro?] [1688]

COLLATION: 29 cm. (fol.): π1 ¶–2¶⁴ A–4F⁴ 4G⁴ (–4G4). [18], 599, [7] p., [3] leaves of plates.

NOTES: Covers through 1563; this is part 1 only of 2 parts projected to cover through 1630; no more was published. Divided into 12 books; there is an added engraved general title page and an added engraved title page prefixed to "Libro primero" and to "Libro tercero." Author's name found on added engraved general title page. Place of publication and printer's name suggested by Peeters-Fontainas. Tax statement (p. [11]) dated 9 Aug. 1688. Errata statement on p. [11]. Three leaves of plates are the three engraved title pages. Preliminary matter includes commendatory poetry by Juan Meléndez, Diego de Figueroa, and Ignacio Martinez de Aibar.

REFERENCES: J. C. Brown, Cat., 1482–1700, II:1364; Medina, *Bib. hispano-americana*, 1816; Sabin, 62704; Palau y Dulcet (2nd ed.), 89568; Peeters-Fontainas, *Bib. des impressions espagnoles*, 455.

JCB LIBRARY COPY: Acquired in 1846. Bound in contemporary calf.

COPIES: MWA, OCU, PPL, RPJCB, NNH, NHi, DPU, CU, DLC, NBuU, InU, MiU-C, WU, MdBP, ICN, NN, TxU, CtY.

## 67

FLORES, BARTOLOMÉ DE.

Obra nueuamente compuesta, en la qual se cue[n]ta, la felice victoria que Dios por su infinita bondad y misericordia, fue seruido de dar, al . . . Pedro Melendez . . . Contra Iuan Ribao . . . Con otros mil Luteranos, a los quales passo à filo de espada, co[n] otras curiosidades que pone el auctor, de las viuiendas de los Indios dela Florida, y sus naturales fayciones. Co[m]puesta en verso castellano, por Barthòlome de Flores . . .

Fue impressa en Seuilla en casa de Hernando Diaz . . . a la calle de la Sierpe. Año de mil y quinientos y setenta y vno. [1571]

COLLATION: 20 cm. (4to): [8] p.

NOTES: Illustrated title page. Publication statement from colophon. Leaves unsigned.

REFERENCES: Alden, *European Americana*, 571/12.

JCB LIBRARY COPY: Acquired in 1940.

COPIES: RPJCB.

## 74

GARCÍA, GREGORIO, d. 1627.

Origen de los Indios de el Nueuo Mundo, e Indias Occidentales. Aueriguado con discurso de opiniones por el padre presentado fray Gregorio Garcia de la Orden de Predicadores. Tratanse en este libro varias cosas, y puntos curiosos, tocantes a diuersas ciencias y facultades, con que se haze varia historia, de mucho gusto para el ingenio y entendimiento de hombres agudos y curiosos. . . .

En Valencia, en casa de Pedro Patricio Mey, junto a San Martin. M.DC.VII. [1607]

COLLATION: 16 cm. (8vo): †⁸ 2†⁴ A–2M⁸ χ². [24], 535, [29] p.; ill.

NOTES: Includes index.

REFERENCES: JCB Lib. cat., pre-1675, II, p. 44; Alden, *European Americana*, 607/35.

JCB LIBRARY COPY: Acquired in 1852. Pages 457–458 and [26–29] repaired with slight losses of text.

COPIES: DLC, NcD, MiU-C, CtY, MB, InU, NHi, NN, RPJCB.

## 52

GRIJALVA, JUAN DE, 1580–1638.

Crónica de la orden de N. P. S. Augustín en las prouincias de la Nueua España en quatro edades desde el año de .1533 hasta el de .1592 por el. P. M. F. Ioan de Grijalua prior del conuento de N. P. S. Augustin de Mexíco.
Mexico. En el religiosissimo conuento de S. Augustin, y imprenta de Ioan Ruyz. Año de 1624.

COLLATION: 28 cm. (fol.): +⁴ A–3K⁴. [4], 218, [6] leaves.

NOTES: At head of title: IHS. Engraved title page. Publication statement from colophon. Errata statement on leaf [3] recto, 1st count. Includes index.

REFERENCES: JCB Lib. cat., pre-1675, II, p. 186; Sabin, 28845, 17606; Medina, *México*, 368; Palau y Dulcet (2nd ed.), 109031; Streit, *Bib. missionum*, II:1552.

JCB LIBRARY COPIES: Copy 1 acquired in 1944. This copy is closely cropped at top and outer edges affecting title page and some text. Copy 2 acquired in 1846. This copy lacks title page which is available in facsimile, contains contemporary [?] ms. annotations, and has leaf 81 misbound after leaf 82.

COPIES: DLC, CU-B, NNH, InU, NNAHi, WU, LNHT, TxU, PPL, CtY, RPJCB.

## 46

HERRERA Y TORDESILLAS, ANTONIO DE, d. 1625.

Historia general de los hechos de los castellanos en las islas i Tierra Firme del Mar Oceano escrita por Antonio de Herrera coronista mayor de Su Md: de las Indias y su coronista de Castilla . . . Decada primera [-octaua].

En Mad: [i.e. Madrid] en la Emplenta Real, 1601–[1615]

COLLATION: 30 cm. (fol.): v. 1: 2¶⁴ A–V⁸ Z¹⁰ ¶⁸ ²2¶²; v. 2: π² 2A–2Z⁸ §⁸; v. 3: π² a–z⁸ 2a⁶ 2§⁸ (2a6 blank); v. 4: π² 2A–2R⁸ 2S¹⁰ §⁸ (§8 blank); v. 5: π² A–F⁸; v. 6: ¶⁴ A–V⁸ ²¶¹⁰ (V8 blank); v. 7: ¶² 2A–2T⁸ 2¶⁸; v. 8: ¶⁴ A–T⁸ V⁶ 3¶¹⁰; v. 9: ¶⁴ 2A–2T⁸ 2V¹⁰ 4§⁸ (2V10 blank). Vol. 1: [8], 371, [21] p.; v. 2: [4], 368, [16] p.; v. 3: [4], 377, [19] p.; v. 4: [4], 258, 261–293, [17] p.; v. 5: [4], 96 p., 14 folded leaves of plates; v. 6: [8], 317, [23] p.; v. 7: [4], 302, [18] p.; v. 8: [8], 315, [21] p.; v. 9: [8], 256, 277–341, [19] p.; maps.

NOTES: On title page of v. 1: En quatro decades desde el año de .1492. hasta el de 1531. Colophons of v. 2–5 read: En Madrid, por Iuan Flamenco. Año M.DCI; colophons of v. 7–9 read: En Madrid. Por Iuan de la Cuesta. Año de M.DC.XV. Each volume has engraved title page (v. 1, 3, 5 and 6 with imprint at bottom). Numerous errors in paging. 9v. bound as 4. Vols. 1–4 contain the first 4 decades; v. 5 is the "Descripcion de las Indias Ocidentales"; v. 6–9 contain the last 4 decades, continuing the history from 1532 to 1554. Errata statement on p. [4], 1st count, of v. 6. Each decade has a separate index.

REFERENCES: JCB Lib. cat., pre-1675, II, p. 9; Alden, *European Americana*, 601/42; Medina, *Bib. hispano-americana*, 455; Palau y Dulcet (2nd ed.), 114286.

JCB LIBRARY COPIES: Copy 1 acquired in 1854. In this copy, v. 4 lacks last leaf (blank); "Tabla de la quarta decada" is misbound at end of v. 5; v. 5 has part of blank leaf inserted between p. 58–59; this copy printed on thicker paper. Copy 2 acquired in 1915. In this copy, v. 1 lacks p. [3–6], 1st count; v. 3 lacks leaf 2a6 (blank); v. 4 lacks last leaf (blank); v. 6 lacks leaf V8 (blank); v. 9 lacks leaf 2V10 (blank).

COPIES: NN, CU-B, NIC, MH, InU, LNHT, MiU-C, ViU, PBL, MnU, CU, RPJCB, NNH, NjP.

## 56

JARQUE, FRANCISCO, 1609–1691.

Insignes missioneros de la Compañia de Jesus en la provincia del Paraguay. Estado presente de sus missiones en Tucumàn, Paraguay, y Rio de la Plata, que comprehende su districo. Por el Doct. D. Francisco Xarque . . . Que remite, y consagra à los religiosos operarios, y apostolicos missioneros, que al presente prosiguen sus heroycas empressas, por mano del Rmo. P. y sapientissimo doctor el padre Thirso

Gonçalez de Santalla, preposito general, y atlante de las missiones que por todo el orbe exercita la religion amplissima de la Compañia de Jesus.

En Pamplona, por Juan Micòn, impressor. Año 1687.

COLLATION: 22 cm. (4to): ¶–2¶⁴ χ⁴ A–2D⁸ (2D8 blank). [24], 217, 220–432, [2] p.

NOTES: Errata statement on p. [22–23]. Contents: book 1, the life of Simon Maceta.—Book 2, the life of Francisco Diaz Taño.—Book 3, "El estado que al presente gozan las missiones . . ."

REFERENCES: J. C. Brown, Cat., 1482–1700, II:1345; Sabin, 105716; Medina, *Bib. hispano-americana*, 1808; Streit, *Bib. missionum*, II:2236; Backer-Sommervogel, XI, col. 1349.

JCB LIBRARY COPY: Acquired in 1846. Lacks last leaf (blank).

COPIES: DLC, InU, PPL, NN, RPJCB.

## 66

LASSO DE LA VEGA, GABRIEL, 1559 – c. 1615.

Primera parte de Cortés valeroso, y Mexicana, de Gabriel Lasso de la Vega . . .

En Madrid, en casa de Pedro Madrigal, año M.D.LXXXVIII. [1588]

COLLATION: 21 cm. (4to): *⁸ A–2B⁸ (2B8 verso blank). [8], 193, [7] leaves; coats of arms, ports.

NOTES: In verse. Colophon reads: En Madrid a deziocho de Diziembre, de M.D.LXXXVII. Años. Errata statement at end.

REFERENCES: JCB Lib. cat., pre-1675, I, p. 313; Alden, *European Americana*, 588/55; Medina, *Bib. hispano-americana*, 316.

JCB LIBRARY COPY: Acquired in 1846.

COPIES: DLC, ICN, RPJCB, NN, MH, NNH.

## 22

Libro vltimo del summario delle Indie Occidentali.

In Vinegia, MDXXXIII. [1534]

COLLATION: 21 cm. (4to): A–D⁴ (D3 verso, D4 blank). [32] p.

NOTES: Translation of: La conquista del Peru. Seville, 1534. Caption title reads: Libro vltimo del summario de le cose de le Indie Occidentali, doue si narra di tutto quello ch'è stato fatto nel trouar la prouincia de Peru, ouer del Cusco, chiamata hoggi Nuoua Castiglia, dalli capitani del imperatore. Issued as a part of: Summario de la generale historia de l'Indie Occidentali, a collection of three works compiled and edited by Giovanni Battista Ramusio. Title and date of publication taken from half title leaf; place of publication taken from colophon at end.

REFERENCES: Cf. JCB Lib. cat., pre-1675, I, p. 114; cf. Alden, *European Americana*, 534/28; cf. Church, *Discovery*, 69; cf. Medina, *Bib. hispano-americana*, 75n.

JCB LIBRARY COPY: Acquired in 1846.

COPIES: NNH, DLC, MiU-C, NN, NjP, ViU, MiU, MnU, IU, RPJCB, ICN, NNC, MH, InU, CtY.

## 34

LOPEZ DE COGOLLUDO, DIEGO, c. 1612–1665.

Historia de Yucathan. Compuesta por el M. R. P. Fr. Diego Lopez Cogolludo, lector jubilado, y padre perpetuo de dicha prouincia. . . . Sacala a luz el M. R. P. Fr. Francisco de Ayeta, predicador . . .

En Madrid: por Juan Garcia Infanzon, año 1688.

COLLATION: 30 cm. (fol.): π² ¶⁶ 2¶⁸ A–3V⁶ (π2, 3V6 verso blank). [32], 760, [32] p.; ill.

NOTES: Added engraved title page reads: Historia de la prouincia de Yucathan . . . Author el R. P. F. Juan [*sic*] Lopez de Cogolludo. Errata statement on p. [31], 1st count. Includes index.

REFERENCES: Palau y Dulcet (2nd ed.), 141001; Medina, *Bib. hispano-americana*, 1821; Sabin, 14210; Streit, *Bib. missionum*, II:2245.

JCB LIBRARY COPY: Acquired in 1942.

COPIES: DLC, OC, InU, CU-B, NcD, NN, RPJCB, NNH.

## 9 and 42

LÓPEZ DE GÓMARA, FRANCISCO, 1511–1564.

La istoria de las Indias. y Conquista de Mexico. 1552.

Fue impressa . . . en casa de Agustin Millan. y acabose vispera de Nauidad año de mil y quinientos y cinquenta y dos en la muy noble y leal ciudad de Çaragoça. [1552]

COLLATION: 30 cm. (fol.): π² a–z⁴ A–G⁴ ²a–²z⁴ ²A–

M⁴. cxxij, cxxxix, [1] leaves, [2] folded leaves of plates; 2 maps.

NOTES: Author's name from verso of title leaf: Francisco Lopez de Gomara . . . excriue la presente istoria . . . Publication statement from colophon. Illustrated title pages (royal arms of Spain). Some errors in paging. "La conquista de Mexico" (leaves [i]–cxxxix) has special title page, and separate foliation and signatures. Errata statement on leaf cxxij recto, 1st count. Contains a brief list of Aztec words on leaves cxvij verso–cxix recto, 2nd count.

REFERENCES: Alden, *European Americana*, 552/22; Wagner, *Spanish Southwest*, 2.

JCB LIBRARY COPY: Acquired in 1940. This copy has a duplicate of leaf ²a4. A cancel slip "rei de Tezcuco" is pasted on leaf ³o1 recto, beneath heading of 2nd column.

COPIES: InU, RPJCB.

### 53

MELÉNDEZ, JUAN, *fl.* 1681.

Tesoros verdaderos de las Yndias en la historia de la gran prouincia de San Iuan Bautista del Peru de el Orden de Predicadores al reuerendissimo padre F. Antonio de Monroy mexicano, general del dicho orden. Por el maestro F. Iuan Melendez natural de Lima, hijo de la misma prouincia, y su coronista . . .

En Roma, en la imprenta de Nicolas Angel Tinassio. M.DC.LXXXI–[M.DC.LXXXII] [1681–1682]

COLLATION: 30 cm. (fol.): v. 1: π1 [a]⁴ b–d⁴ e⁶ A–4N⁴ 4O⁶ (4O6 verso blank); v. 2: π1 [a]⁴ b⁸ A–4P⁴ 4Q⁸; v. 3: π1 [a]⁴ b–c⁶ A–5Q⁴ 5R⁶. Vol. 1: [46], 643, [25] p., [4] leaves of plates (3 folded); ill., port., plan; v. 2: [26], 669, [19] p., [1] leaf of plates; v. 3: [34], 857, [19] p., [1] leaf of plates.

NOTES: Vol. 2 has different title page with same imprint: . . . De el Orden de Predicadores al M. R. P. maestro F. Enrique de Guzman prouincial de Tierra Santa, compañero de N. Reuerendissimo. Por el P. maestro . . . Vol. 3 has different title page: . . . De el Orden de Predicadores al M. R. P. maestro Fr. Iuan delos Rios su prouincial a la misma prouincia Peruana y en su lugar al M. R. P. maestro Fr. Lorenzo Muñoz compañero de Nuestro Reuerendissimo. Por el P. maestro . . . En Roma . . . M.DC.LXXXII. Includes indexes. Title vignettes: coats of arms of dedicatees. Each volume has added engraved title page and half title.

REFERENCES: J. C. Brown, Cat., 1482–1700, II:1220; Sabin, 47423; Medina, *Bib. hispano-americana*, 1717; Palau y Dulcet (2nd ed.), 160165.

JCB LIBRARY COPY: Acquired before 1874. This copy imperfect: portrait and engraved title pages in v. 2–3 wanting; available in facsimile.

COPIES: RPJCB, CtY, NN, DLC, PBL, InU, OrU, MiU, NNH, MWA, CU-B.

### 45

MONARDES, NICOLÁS, *c.* 1512–1588.

Dos libros. El vno trata de todas las cosas q[ue] trae[n] de n[uest]ras Indias Occide[n]tales, que siruen al vso de medicina . . . El otro libro, trata de dos medicinas marauillosas q[ue] son co[n]tra todo veneno . . . Con la cura delos venenados. . . . Agora nueuamente co[m]puestos por el doctor Niculoso de Monardes medico de Seuilla . . .

Seuilla, en casa de Sebastian Trugillo. Acabose a diez y seys dias del mes de iunio. 1565.

COLLATION: 15 cm. (8vo): a–q⁸ r⁴ (r4 verso blank). [264] p.

NOTES: Place of publication, printer, and date of publication (except for the year) taken from colophon on p. [261]. Includes index.

REFERENCES: Alden, *European Americana*, 565/45; Guerra, *Monardes*, 7; Medina, *Bib. hispano-americana*, 194.

JCB LIBRARY COPY: Acquired in 1929. This copy is bound in contemporary calf; title page border is hand-colored. Also in this copy, the number "51" in manuscript appears on the title page before the word "marauedis".

COPIES: NN, RPJCB, DNLM.

### 40

MORGA, ANTONIO DE, 1559–1636.

Sucesos de las islas Filipinas. . . . Por el doctor Antonio de Morga, alcalde del crimen, de la Real Audiencia de la Nueua España, consultor del Santo Oficio de la Inquisicion.

En Mexico. En casa de Geronymo Balli. Año 1609. Por Cornelio Adriano Cesar.

COLLATION: 20 cm. (4to): §⁶ A–2V⁴. [6], 172 leaves.

NOTES: Leaves 4, 6, 15, 16 misnumbered 5, 5, 16, 15. Some copies have engraved title page; cf. Retana. Title vignette: coat of arms.

REFERENCES: JCB Lib. cat., pre-1675, II, p. 64; Medina, *México*, 249; Sabin, 50631; Retana, *Aparato bib. de la historia general de Filipinas*, 68.

JCB LIBRARY COPY: Acquired in 1846. This copy has letterpress title page.

COPIES: NN, RPJCB.

## 32

NÚÑEZ CABEZA DE VACA, ALVAR, 16th cent.

La relacion que dio Aluar Nuñez Cabeça de Vaca de lo acaescido enlas Indias enla armada donde yua por gouernador Pa[m]philo de Narbaez \ desde el año de veynte y siete hasta el año d[e] treynta y seys que boluio a Seuilla con tres de su compañia.

Fue impressa . . . en . . . Zamora: por . . . Augustin de Paz y Juan Picardo . . . A costa y espensas del virtuoso varon Juan Pedro Musetti . . . de Medina del Campo. [1542]

COLLATION: 21 cm. (4to): A–H⁸ I⁴ (–I4) (I3 verso blank). [134] p.

NOTES: Publication statement from colophon which is dated: Acabose en seys dias del mes de octubre. Año del nasçimiento d[e] N[uest]ro Saluador Jesu Cristo de mil y quinientos y quarenta y dos años. Illustrated title page: coat of arms of Spain.

REFERENCES: Alden, *European Americana*, 542/21; Medina, *Bib. hispano-americana*, 114; Wagner, *Spanish Southwest*, 1.

JCB LIBRARY COPY: Acquired in 1929. Bound in contemporary vellum, and lacks p. [13–14] which have been replaced in facsimile.

COPIES: NN, RPJCB.

## 63

OÑA, PEDRO DE, 1570?–1643?

Primera parte de Arauco domado, compuesto por el licenciado Pedro de Oña. . . .

Impresso en la Ciudad delos Reyes [Lima], por Antonio Ricardo de Turin. . . . Año de 1596.

COLLATION: 21 cm. (4to): ¶¹² A–X⁸ ²X⁴ Y–2T⁸ 2V⁴ (2V4 verso blank). [12], 70, 70–77, 76–139 [i.e. 133], 133–164, [4], 165–335, [1] leaves; port.

NOTES: In verse. No more parts ever published. Errata statement on leaf [2] verso, 1st count.

REFERENCES: JCB Lib. cat., pre-1675, I, p. 347; Sabin, 57300; Medina, *Lima*, 10.

JCB LIBRARY COPY: Acquired in 1846. Lacks leaf [12], 1st count; available in facsimile.

COPIES: NN, NNH, RPJCB, InU, MB.

## 71

ORDOÑEZ DE CEVALLOS, PEDRO, b. 1550?

Viage del mundo. Hecho y compuesto por el licenciado Pedro Ordoñez de Ceuallos, natural de la insigne ciudad de Iaen. Contiene tres libros. . . .

En Madrid, por Luis Sanchez impressor del Rey N. S. Año M.DC.XIIII. [1614]

COLLATION: 20 cm. (4to): ¶² 2¶⁸ A–2N⁸ 2O⁴ 2P² (2P2 verso blank). [10], 290, [4] leaves; port.

NOTES: Several leaves misnumbered. Title vignette: arms of don Antonio Davila y Toledo. Includes accounts of the author's voyages to Spanish South America.

REFERENCES: JCB Lib. cat., pre-1675, II, p. 104; Alden, *European Americana*, 614/82; Medina, *Bib. hispano-americana*, 609.

JCB LIBRARY COPY: Acquired in 1915. Bound in contemporary vellum.

COPIES: NN, RPJCB, MnU, NNH, InU, CtY.

## 38

OVALLE, ALONSO DE, 1601–1651.

Historica relacion del reyno de Chile, y delas missiones, y ministerios que exercita en el la Compañia de Iesus. . . . Alonso de Oualle de la Compañia de Iesus . . .

En Roma, por Francisco Cauallo. M.DC.XLVI. [1646]

COLLATION: 27 cm. (fol.): π1 §⁴ A–3L⁴. [10], 455, [1] p., [38] leaves of plates (1 folded), 12, 6 p. of plates; ill., maps, plans, ports.

NOTES: Half title reads: Varias, y curiosas noticias del reino de Chile. In eight books. Page 51 misnumbered 31. The engraved plates between p. 322 and 323 have two separate title pages: in one state these two title pages are printed in large letterpress capitals; in the other state these title pages are engraved instead of printed. Errata statement on p. 455. Includes index.

REFERENCES: JCB Lib. cat., pre-1675, II, p. 345; Alden, *European Americana,* 646/112; Medina, *Bib. hispano-chilena,* 118; Wroth, L. C. "Alonso de Ovalle's large map of Chile, 1646." *Imago Mundi* XVI (1959): 90–95.

JCB LIBRARY COPIES: Copy 1 acquired in 1917. This copy has the large folded map referred to by Wroth as Tabula A, and the two separate title pages of the first state described. Copy 2 acquired in 1846. This copy lacks the half title leaf, and has the smaller folded map referred to by Wroth as Tabula B. It is the map most commonly found with this work. This copy has the two separate title pages of the second state described.

COPIES: PPL, NN, NjR, DLC, RPJCB, NIC, CtU, MoSU, MnU, InU, CU.

## 58

PARRA, JACINTO DE, 17th cent.

Rosa laureada entre los santos. Epitalamios sacros de la corte, aclamaciones de España, aplausos de Roma, congratulaciones festivas del clero, y religiones, al feliz desposorio que celebro en la gloria con Christo la Beata Virgen Rosa de Santa Maria, de la tercera orden de Predicadores, patrona del Perù, beatificacion solemne que promulgo en la iglesia militante la Santidad de Clemente Nono, de felize recordacion, en 15. de abril de 1668. . . . El muy R. P. M. Fr. Iacinto de Parra, Matritense, de la Orden de Santo Domingo . . .

En Madrid: por Domingo Garcia Morrás, impressor del estado eclesiastico de la corona de Castilla, y Leon. Año de 1670.

COLLATION: 29 cm. (fol.): ¶⁶ 2¶⁴ A–3E⁶ 3F⁸ 3G–3O⁶ 3P⁸ (3P8 verso blank). [20], 651, [89] p., [1] leaf of plates; port.

NOTES: Errata statement on p. [19], 1st count. Includes index.

REFERENCES: JCB Lib. cat., pre-1675, III, p. 205; Medina, *Bib. hispano-americana,* 1491; Streit, *Bib. missionum,* II:2050; Sabin, 58838.

JCB LIBRARY COPY: Acquired in 1909. This copy lacks the portrait, p. [3–18], 1st count, and p. 409–410; title page is torn with some loss of text and mounted; p. [76–89], 203, 204 are torn with some losses of text.

COPIES: NN, RPJCB.

## 59

PIZARRO Y ORELLANA, FERNANDO, d. 1652?

Varones ilustres del Nuevo Mundo. Descubridores, conquistadores, y pacificadores del opulento, dilatado, y poderoso imperio de las Indias Occidentales: sus vidas, virtud, valor, hazañas, y claros blasones. Ilustrados en los sucessos destas vidas con singulares observaciones politicas, morales, iuridicas, miscelaneas, y razon de estado; para mayor autoridad de la historia, y demonstracion della, y su utilissima leccion. Con un discurso legal de la obligacion que tienen los reyes a premiar los servicios de sus vassallos; ò en ellos, ò en sus descendientes. . . . Escrive don Fernando Pizarro y Orellana, cavallero de la Orden de Calatrava . . . Lleva seis indices, ò sumarios: uno de autores: otro de leyes: otro de capitulos: otro de observaciones: otro de lugares de escritura: y otro de cosas memorables; para mas facil comprehension de toda la obra.

En Madrid, por Diego Diaz de la Carrera. Año M.DC.XXXIX. A costa de Pedro Coello mercader de libros. [1639]

COLLATION: 29 cm. (fol.): ¶¹⁰ 2¶²·²¶⁶ A–2M⁶ 2N⁴ a–f⁶ ²A⁶ ²B1–4+. [36], 427, [1], 72, [32] p.

NOTES: Numerous errors in paging. Contents: Vida del almirante don Cristoval Colon—Vida del capitan Alonso de Ojeda—Vida de Fernan Cortes—Vida del marques don Francisco Pizarro—Vida de Iuan Pizarro—Vida del mariscal don Diego de Almagro—Vida de Hernando Pizarro—Vida de Gonzalo Pizarro—Vida del maestre de campo Diego Garcia de Paredes—Discurso legal y politico. "Discurso legal y politico," 72 p. (preceding indexes) was also published separately as: Discurso . . . en que se muestra la obligacion qui Su Magestad tiene . . . a cumplir . . . [Madrid, probably between 1630 and 1640].

REFERENCES: JCB Lib. cat., pre-1675, II, p. 276; Alden, *European Americana,* 639/93; Medina, *Bib. hispano-americana,* 999.

JCB LIBRARY COPY: Acquired in 1846. Lacks p. [21–

32] at end; leaf [D5] closely trimmed at top edge with slight loss of text.

COPIES: DLC, RPJCB, CaBViPa, NN, CtU, MH-P, IaU, MoSW, PPL, OCU, DDO, InU, MoSU, CU, CtY, NcD, LNHT, MWA, NNH, MnU, NcU, MiU-C.

## 8

Relatione di alcune cose della Nuona [sic] Spagna, & della gran città di Temestitan Messico. fatta per vno genlil'homo [sic] del signor Fernando Cortese.

[In Venetia nella stamperia de Giunti. L'anno MDLVI. 1556]

COLLATION: 32 cm. (fol.): 2p8 (verso) 2q1–6 (recto). Leaves 304 verso–310 recto; ill., plan.

NOTES: Caption title. Issued as a part of Ramusio's: Terzo volume delle nauigationi et viaggi. Venice, 1556. Translation from a Spanish manuscript.

REFERENCES: Cf. JCB Lib. cat., pre-1675, I, p. 194; cf. Alden, *European Americana*, 556/38; cf. Church, *Discovery*, 99.

JCB LIBRARY COPIES: Copy 1 acquired before 1854; copy 2 acquired in 1906.

COPIES: NIC, OC, MH, InU, MWiW-C, IU, MnU, DLC, DFo, CtY, ICN, RPJCB, CaBVaU, MU, IaU, NcD, PBL.

## 51

REMESAL, ANTONIO DE, b. c. 1570.

Historia general de las Indias Ocidentales, y particular de la gouernacion de Chiapa, y Guatemala. Escriuese juntamente los principios de la religion de nuestro glorioso padre Santo Domingo, y de las demas religiones.... Por el presentado fray Antonio de Remesal...

En Madrid, por Francisco de Abarca. Año M.DC.XX. [1620]

COLLATION: 30 cm. (fol.): π⁶ A–2T⁸ 3A–3G⁸ 3H⁶. [12], 784 [i.e. 796] p.

NOTES: Originally published in 1619 as: Historia de la prouincia de S. Vicente de Chyapa y Guatemala. Colophon reads: En Madrid, por Francisco de Angulo. Año de 1619. Errata statement on leaf π2 verso.

REFERENCES: JCB Lib. cat., pre-1675, II, p. 140; Alden, *European Americana*, 620/131; Medina, *Bib. hispano-americana*, 704; Palau y Dulcet (2nd ed.), 260794.

JCB LIBRARY COPY: Acquired before 1854. This copy contains, in addition to the printed title page, the engraved title page of the 1619 edition. Pages 407–414 are misbound.

COPIES: NN, MH-P, IMunS, MWA, MH, DLC, RPJCB.

## 36

RODRÍGUEZ, MANUEL, 1633–1701.

El Marañon, y Amazonas. Historia de los descubrimientos, entradas, y reduccion de naciones. Trabajos malogrados de algunos conquistadores, y dichosos de otros, assi temporales, como espirituales, en las dilatadas montañas, y mayores rios de la America. Escrita por el padre Manuel Rodriguez, de la Compañia de Iesus, procurador general de las prouincias de Indias, en la corte de Madrid....

En Madrid, en la imprenta de Antonio Gonçalez de Reyes. Año de 1684.

COLLATION: 30 cm. (fol.): ¶–2¶⁶ A–2O⁶ *–2*⁶ 2P⁴ (2P4 verso blank). [24], 444, [24], [8] p.

NOTES: With (as issued?) his: Compendio historial, e indice chronologico Peruano, y del nueuo reyno de Granada... [Madrid, 1684], with separate paging and signatures (p. [1–24], 3rd count). Contains extensive extracts from Cristóbal de Acuña's: Nueuo descubrimiento del gran río de las Amazonas, Madrid, 1641 (p. 101–141, 425–428). Errata statement on p. [16], 1st count.

REFERENCES: J. C. Brown, Cat., 1482–1700, II:1297; Sabin, 72524; Medina, *Bib. hispano-americana*, 1771; Palau y Dulcet (2nd ed.), 273201; Streit, *Bib. missionum*, II:2201; Backer-Sommervogel, VI, col. 1965.

JCB LIBRARY COPY: Acquired in 1840. Lacks half title leaf; available in facsimile.

COPIES: InU, NIC, MnU, NBuU, ICN, NNH, DLC, DPU, NcD, CtY, NN, MB, RPJCB, NHi, WU.

## 55

RUIZ DE MONTOYA, ANTONIO, 1585–1652.

Conquista espiritual hecha por los religiosos de la Compañia de Iesus, en las prouincias del Paraguay,

Parana, Vruguay, y Tape. Escrita por el padre Antonio Ruiz de la misma compañia. . . .

Año 1639. En Madrid. En la imprenta del reyno.

COLLATION: 21 cm. (4to): †⁴ A–N⁸ (N8 verso blank). [4], 103, [1] leaves.

NOTES: Title vignette: Jesuit trigram. Errata statement on leaf [2] verso. Includes index.

REFERENCES: JCB Lib. cat., pre-1675, II, p. 277; Alden, *European Americana*, 639/100; Fúrlong Cárdiff, *Antonio Ruiz de Montoya*, 29.

JCB LIBRARY COPY: Acquired in 1846.

COPIES: DLC, InU, WU, NIC, MnU, MWA, PU, ICN, RPJCB, NN, NNH.

## 21

SÁNCHEZ DE AGUILAR, PEDRO, 1555–1648.

Informe contra idolorum cultores del obispado de Yucatan. . . . Por el doctor don Pedro Sanchez de Aguilar . . .

En Madrid. Por la viuda de Iuan Gonçalez, año de M.DC.XXXIX. [1639]

COLLATION: 21 cm. (4to): ¶–2¶⁴ A–2H⁴ (2H4 verso blank). [8], 124 leaves.

NOTES: Text in Spanish and Latin. Title vignette: coat of arms.

REFERENCES: JCB Lib. cat., pre-1675, II, p. 277; Alden, *European Americana*, 639/105.

JCB LIBRARY COPY: Acquired in 1846.

COPIES: TxU, RPJCB, CtY.

## 24

SANCHO, PEDRO.

Relatione per Sua Maesta di quel che nel conquisto & pacificatione di queste prouincie della Nuoua Castiglia è successo, & della qualità del paese dopo che il capitano Fernando Pizarro si partì & ritorno à Sua Maesta. Il rapporto del conquistamento di Caxamalca & la prigione del Cacique Atabalipa.

[In Venetia nella stamperia di Giunti. L'anno MDLVI. 1556]

COLLATION: 32 cm. (fol.): 3d4 (verso)–3d8 3e⁸ χ² 3f1–2. Leaves 398 verso–414 verso; plan.

NOTES: Sancho's name appears at end. Caption title.

Issued as a part of Ramusio's: Terzo volume delle nauigationi et viaggi. Venice, 1556. Translated from a Spanish manuscript. Gathering "χ" is a double plate depicting a plan of the city of Cusco (numbered as leaves 411–412).

REFERENCES: Cf. JCB Lib. cat., pre-1675, I, p. 194; cf. Alden, *European Americana*, 556/38; cf. Church, *Discovery*, 99.

JCB LIBRARY COPIES: Copy 1 acquired before 1854; copy 2 acquired in 1906.

COPIES: NIC, OC, MH, InU, MWiW-C, IU, MnU, DLC, DFo, CtY, ICN, RPJCB, CaBVaU, MU, IaU, NcD, PBL.

## 39

SARMIENTO DE GAMBOA, PEDRO, 1532?–1608?

Viage al Estrecho de Magallanes por el capitan Pedro Sarmiento de Gambóa en los años de 1579. y 1580. y noticia de la expedicion que despues hizo para poblarle.

En Madrid: en la Imprenta Real de la Gazeta. Año de 1768.

COLLATION: 24 cm. (4to): a–k⁴ l² ²a–3h⁴ 3i⁴ (–3i4) (3i3 verso blank). LXXXIV, 402, [2], xxxiii, [1] p., [3] folded leaves of plates; ill.

NOTES: "The journal of the voyage of Sarmiento de Gamboa is here printed for the first time from the original manuscript, preserved in the Royal Library at Madrid. It was edited by Don Bernardo Yriarte"—Sabin. "Compendio del derrotero de Pedro Sarmiento que Bartolomé Leonardo de Argensola sacó y publicó en su historia de las Malucas . . . ": p. XXXIX–LXX. "Testimonios de varios autores que hacen mencion de Pedro Sarmiento": p. LXXI–LXXVIII. "Carta del virréi del Perú don Francisco de Toledo al gobernador del Rio-de-la-Plata . . .": p. LXXIX–LXXXIV. "Declaracion que . . . hizo, ante escribano, Tomé Hernandez, de lo sucedido en las dos poblaciones fundadas en el Estrecho de Magallánes por Pedro Sarmiento de Gambóa": xxxii p. at end. Includes index.

REFERENCES: J. C. Brown, Cat., 1493–1800, II:1638; Medina, *Bib. hispano-chilena*, 482; Sabin, 77094; Palau y Dulcet (2nd ed.), 302364.

JCB LIBRARY COPY: Acquired before 1870. Half bound in contemporary calf with marble boards.

COPIES: MB, RPJCB, DLC, NNH, ICN, MWA, InU, CU-S, CtY, CU, PPL, NN.

## 12

SOLÍS, ANTONIO DE, 1610–1686.

Historia de la conquista de Mexico, poblacion, y progressos de la America Septentrional, conocida por el nombre de Nueva España. Escriviala don Antonio de Solis, secretario de Su Magestad, y su chronista mayor de las Indias. . . .

En Madrid. En la imprenta de Bernardo de Villa-Diego, impressor de Su Magestad. Año M.DC.LXXXIV. [1684]

COLLATION: 30 cm. (fol.): ¶–2¶⁸ A–2L⁸ 2M⁶ 2N⁴ (2N4 verso blank). [32], 548, [16] p., [1] leaf of plates.

NOTES: Added engraved title page reads: Historia de la Nueva España . . . Theod. Ardeman inv. I F Leonardo sculp. Includes index. Errata statement on p. [21].

REFERENCES: J. C. Brown, Cat., 1482–1700, II:1300; Sabin, 86446; Palau y Dulcet (2nd ed.), 318602; Medina, *Bib. hispano-americana*, 1773.

JCB LIBRARY COPY: Acquired in 1854.

COPIES: MiU-C, MB, RPJCB, CU-B, CLCM, DLC, DFº, MH-P, OC, InU, TxU, CtY, CU-S, MiU, CU-A.

## 48

SOLÓRZANO PEREIRA, JUAN DE, 1575–1655.

Ioannes de Solorzano Pereira I. V. D. . . . Disputationem de Indiarum iure, sive De iusta Indiarum Occidentalium inquisitione, acquisitione, et retentione tribus libris comprehensam, D. E. C. . . .

Matriti. Ex typographia Francisci Martinez. Anno 1629 [–1639]

COLLATION: 35 cm. (fol.): v. 1: ¶⁸ 2¶⁶ A–3F⁸ 3G¹⁰; v. 2: ¶–3¶⁸ 4¶⁴ A–3M⁸ 3N⁶ 3O–3V⁸ 3X–3Y⁶ 3Z–4F⁸ 4G–4H⁶ (4H6 verso blank). Vol. 1: [28], 751, [101] p.; v. 2: [56], 1076, [136] p., [2] leaves of plates; ports.

NOTES: Title page of v. 2 reads: D. Ioannes de Solorzano Pereira I. V. D. . . . Tome alterum de Indiarum iure, sive De justa Indiarum Occidentalium gubernatione quinque libris comprehensum, D. E. C. Matriti. Ex typographia Francisco Martinez. Anno 1639. First Spanish version printed at Madrid in 1648 with title: Politica indiana. Engraved title pages. Numerous errors in paging. Errata statements in v. 1, p. [6], 1st count, and in v. 2, p. [8], 1st count. Includes index.

REFERENCES: JCB Lib. cat., pre-1675, II, p. 224, 278; Alden, *European Americana*, 629/136, 639/112; Medina, *Bib. hispano-americana*, 863, 1006.

JCB LIBRARY COPY: Acquired in 1854. Vol. 1 is trimmed to 30 cm.

COPIES: MiU-C, CSmH, MH-P, OCU, InU, CaBViPA, DLC, NjP, RPJCB, NN, DCU, NNH, IaU, PU, CtY, MH.

## 61

SUÁREZ DE FIGUEROA, CRISTÓBAL, c. 1571–1645.

Hechos de don Garcia Hurtado de Mendoza, quarto marques de Cañete. . . . Por el doctor Christoual Suarez de Figueroa.

En Madrid, en la Imprenta Real. Año M.DC.XIII. [1613]

COLLATION: 21 cm. (4to): *² ¶⁶ A–2S⁴. [16], 248, 245–324 p.

NOTES: Title vignette: coat of arms. Errata statement on p. [3]. Contains an account of Hurtado de Mendoza's career as governor of Chile during the Araucanian War.

REFERENCES: JCB Lib. cat., pre-1675, II, p. 100; Alden, *European Americana*, 613/125; Medina, *Bib. hispano-chilena*, 39.

JCB LIBRARY COPY: Acquired in 1846.

COPIES: DLC, InU, TxU, MU, MiU-C, NNH, RPJCB, NN, MB.

## 70

TAMARA, FRANCISCO.

El libro de las costumbres de todas las gentes del mundo, y de las Indias. Traduzido y copilado por el bachiller Francisco Thamara . . .

En Anuers. En casa de Martin Nucio, a la enseña de las dos cigueñas. 1556.

COLLATION: 15 cm. (8vo): A–2X⁸. 349, [3] leaves.

NOTES: In part a translation and rearrangement of Boemus's: Omnium gentium mores, leges et ritus; with the addition of: Suma y breue relacion de todas las Indias y tierras nueuamente descubiertas por gente de España, assi por la parte de Poniente como de Levante, which forms chapters vi–xvij of book 3. Title vignette: printer's device.

REFERENCES: JCB Lib. cat., pre-1675, I, p. 194; Alden, *European Americana*, 556/45; Medina, *Bib. hispano-americana*, 177.

JCB LIBRARY COPY: Acquired about 1854. Lacks leaves 136–160.

COPIES: NN, RPJCB, MB, MH, DLC.

## 50

TORQUEMADA, JUAN DE, *c*. 1557–1664.

Ia [-IIIa] parte de los veynte y vn libros rituales y monarchia yndiana con el origen y guerras de los Yndias Occidentales de sus poblaçones descubrimiento conquista conuersion y otras cosas marauillosas de la mesma tierra distribuydos en tres tomos compuesto por fray Iuan de Torquemada ministro prouincial de la orden de . . . S. Francisco en . . . Mexico en la Nueba Espana.

En Seuilla por Matthias Clauijo año 1615.

COLLATION: 31 cm. (fol.): v. 1: π1 §² ¶⁸ 2¶⁴ A–3G⁸ 3H–3K² 3L² (–3L2) (3L1 verso blank); v. 2: π1 ¶² §² A–2S⁸ 2T⁶ 2V–2X²; v. 3: π1 §² ¶⁴ A–2X⁸ 2Y⁶ 2Z⁴ 3A² 3C² (3C2 verso blank). Vol. 1: [30], 62, 65–665, 668–844, [22] p.; v.2: [10], 400, 405–464, 467–665, [17] p.; v. 3: [14], 713, [19] p.

NOTES: Each volume has engraved title page. Errata statements in v. 1, leaf §2 verso, v. 2, leaf §1 verso, and v. 3, leaf §1 verso. Includes index at end of each volume.

REFERENCES: JCB Lib. cat., pre-1675, II, p. 109; Alden, *European Americana*, 615/130; Medina, *Bib. hispano-americana*, 634; Streit, *Bib. missionum*, II: 1453.

JCB LIBRARY COPY: Acquired in 1846. Bound in contemporary vellum. Vol. 1 lacks title page which is available in pen and ink facsimile.

COPIES: ICN, RPJCB, CtY.

## 16

TOVAR, JUAN DE, *c*. 1546 – *c*. 1626.

Historia de la benida de los yndios apoblar a Mexico delas partes remotas de Occidente los sucessos y peri-grinaciones del camino su gouierno, ydolos y templos dellos ritos y cirimonias y sacrificios, y sacerdotes dellos fiestas, y bayles, y sus meses y calandarios delos tiempos, los reyes que tuuieron hasta el postrero con otras cosas curiosas sacadas delos archiuos y tradiciones antiguas dellos fecha por el padre Juan de Touar de la Compañia de Iesus inuiada al rey n[uest]ro s[eñor] eneste original de mano escrito.

[Between 1582 and 1587]

COLLATION: 22 cm.: [5], 145, [13] leaves, bound; ill.

NOTES: Probably a holograph. Date of manuscript based on Parry's article; cf. Parry, J. H. "Juan de Tovar and the History of the Indians" (In *Proceedings of the American Philosophical Society*, v. 121, no. 4). Contents: title leaf (verso blank); leaves [2–4] consist of an interchange between Joseph de Acosta and Juan de Tovar concerning the composition of the manuscript; leaf [5] blank; leaves 1–81 comprise the "Historia"; leaves 82–84 blank; leaves 85–140 contain 29 full-page painted illustrations of Mexican scenes, Indian dances, etc., with a numbered blank leaf inserted before each painting; leaf 141 blank; leaf 142 has the calendar wheel; leaf 143 blank; leaves 144–145 contain "los meses"; leaf [1] blank; leaves [2–12] consist of the Aztec calendar coordinated with the Christian one, containing descriptive text and 19 painted illustrations; leaf [13] blank with some manuscript drawings on recto.

JCB LIBRARY COPY: Acquired in 1947.

COPIES: RPJCB.

## 64

VALDÉS, RODRIGO DE, 1609–1682.

Poema heroyco hispano-latino panegyrico de la fundacion, y grandezas de la muy noble, y leal ciudad de Lima. Obra postuma del M. R. P. M. Rodrigo de Valdes, de la Compañia de Jesus, cathedratico de prima jubilado, y prefecto regente de estudios en el Colegio Maximo de San Pablo. Sacala a la luz el doct. D. Francisco Garabito de Leon y Messia, cura-rector de la Iglesia Metropolitana de Lima . . .

En Madrid, en la imprenta de Antonio Roman, año 1687.

COLLATION: 21 cm. (4to): §–7§⁴ a–g⁴ A–2A⁴. [112], 184, [8] p.

NOTES: Preliminary matter includes poetry in part signed by Francisco Cruzado y Aragon, Esteban Cruzado y Ferrer, Francisco Cruzado y Ferrer, and Bartolomé Cruzado. Errata statement on p. [23]. "Carta . . . que escriuiò . . . Francisco del Quadro . . . en la muerte de el Padre Rodrigo de Valdès": p. [57–112].

REFERENCES: J. C. Brown, Cat., 1482–1700, II:1343; Sabin, 98322; Medina, *Bib. hispano-americana,* 1806; Backer-Sommervogel, VIII, col. 376; Palau y Dulcet (2nd ed.), 347681.

JCB LIBRARY COPY: Acquired before 1866.

COPIES: DLC, InU, NcD, NN, RPJCB, NNH, CtY.

## 47

VARGAS MACHUCA, BERNARDO DE, 1557–1622.

Milicia y descripcion de las Indias, por el capitan don Bernardo de Vargas Machuca . . .

En Madrid, en casa de Pedro Madrigal. Año. M.D.XCIX. [1599]

COLLATION: 19 cm. (4to): §–2§⁸ A–2C⁸ (2C7, 2C8 versos blank). [16], 186, [22] leaves; ill., port.

NOTES: Title vignette: coat of arms. Errata statement on leaf [2] verso, 1st count. Includes index.

REFERENCES: JCB Lib. cat., pre-1675, I, p. 377; Alden, *European Americana,* 599/89.

JCB LIBRARY COPY: Acquired before 1865. This copy lacks last leaf, and title page is closely trimmed with loss of imprint date; both are available in facsimile. Leaf 2§8 which contains the portrait is misbound before the title page.

COPIES: DLC, PBL, NN, NCH, InU, MB, RPJCB, NNH, LNHT, MH.

## 33

VEGA, GARCILASO DE LA, 1539–1616.

La Florida del Ynca. Historia del adelantado Hernando de Soto, gouernador y capitan general del reyno de la Florida, y de otros heoicos caualleros españoles è Indios; escrita por el Ynca Garcilasso de la Vega, capitan de Su Magestad, natural de la gran ciudad del Cozco, cabeça de los reynos y prouincias del Peru. . . .

En Lisbona. Impresso por Pedro Crasbeeck. Año 1605.

COLLATION: 20 cm. (4to): ¶¹⁰ A–Z⁸ 2a–2x⁸ 2y⁶ (¶10, 2y6 blank). [10], 351, [7] leaves.

NOTES: There is another issue without the date on the title page.

REFERENCES: JCB Lib. cat., pre-1675, II, p. 31; Alden, *European Americana,* 605/46; Church, *Discovery,* 329; Medina, *Bib. hispano-americana,* 502.

JCB LIBRARY COPY: Acquired in 1846.

COPIES: MiU-C, MWiW-C, ViU, PPL, TxU, MdBP, ICJ, InU, DCU, OCU, CU, NcU, RPJCB, MB, NNH, NHi, NN, OCl, NjP, MB, PBm, NcD, DLC, PP, OU, MiU, MU, OClWHi, KMK, PPFr.

## 30

VEGA, GARCILASO DE LA, 1539–1616.

Primera parte de los commentarios reales, que tratan del origen de los Yncas, reyes que fueron del Peru, de su idolatria, leyes, y gouierno en paz y en guerra: de sus vidas y conquistas, y de todo lo que fue aquel imperio y su republica, antes que los españoles passaran a el. Escritos por el Ynca Garcilasso de la Vega, natural del Cozco, y capitan de Su Magestad. . . .

En Lisboa: en la officina de Pedro Crasbeeck. Año de M.DCIX. [1609]

COLLATION: 27 cm. (fol.): †⁶ 2†⁴ A–2K⁸. [10], 264 leaves, [1] leaf of plates; coat of arms.

NOTES: Colophon reads: En Lisbona. Impresso en casa de Pedro Crasbeeck. Año de MDCVIII. The second part was published at Cordoba, 1616, as: Historia general del Peru. Errata statement on leaf [10] recto.

REFERENCES: JCB Lib. cat., pre-1675, II, p. 61; Alden, *European Americana,* 609/44; Medina, *Bib. hispano-americana,* 549.

JCB LIBRARY COPY: Acquired in 1851.

COPIES: MnU, RPJCB, NNH, PPRF, LNHT, MiU, WaU, ViU, CtY, IEN, MB, MH, MWiW-C, DLC, InU, NN, MBAt, CSmH, NHi, MiU-C, NNC.

## 4

VESPUCCI, AMERIGO, 1451–1512.

Alberic[us] Vespucci[us] Laure[n]tio Petri Francisci de Medicis salutem plurima[m] dicit.

[Paris : F. Baligault and J. Lambert, 1503]

COLLATION: 21 cm. (4to): a⁶ (a6 verso blank). [12] p.; ill.

NOTES: Latin translation by "iocundus interpres" (i.e. Giovanni Giocondo da Verona) of the Italian manuscript giving Vespucci's account of his third voyage. First edition in Latin as described by Sabin. Later published and generally known as: Mundus novus. Title vignette: printer's device. Publication statement taken from Alden. Roman type; 40 lines. Without catchwords and foliation.

REFERENCES: JCB Lib. cat., pre-1675, I, p. 40; Alden, *European Americana*, 503/9; Sabin, 99327; Medina, *Bib. hispano-americana*, 25.

JCB LIBRARY COPY: Acquired in 1854.

COPIES: NN, ViU, NcU, CSmH, MiU-C, RPJCB.

## 65

VILLAGRÁ, GASPAR PÉREZ DE, d. 1620.

Historia de la Nueua Mexico, del capitan Gaspar de Villagra. . . .

Año 1610. En Alcala, por Luys Martinez Grande. A costa de Baptista Lopez mercador de libros.

COLLATION: 15 cm. (8vo): π⁸ ¶–2¶⁸ A–2N⁸ (2N8 verso blank). [24], 287, [1] leaves; port.

NOTES: Thirty-four cantos in blank verse. Title vignette: coat of arms. Errata statement on leaf π3 recto.

REFERENCES: JCB Lib. cat., pre-1675, II, p. 72; Alden, *European Americana*, 610/116; Medina, *Bib. hispano-americana*, 566.

JCB LIBRARY COPY: Acquired in 1846. This copy has mutilated title page with slight loss of text.

COPIES: ICN, MiU-C, CtY, CSmH, NhI, DLC, CU-B, NN, NNH, MH, NjP, InU, DCU, RPJCB.

## 23

XEREZ, FRANCISCO DE, b. 1500.

Uerdadera relacion de la conquista del Peru y prouincia del Cuzco llamada la Nueua Castilla: conquistada por el magnifico y efforçado cauallero Francisco Piçarro . . . embiada a Su Magestad por Francisco de Xerez . . .

Fue vista y examinada esta obra por del arçobispado de Seuilla: [y] impressa en casa de Bartholome Perez en el mes de julio. Año del parto virginal mil [y] quinientos y treynta y quatro. [1534]

COLLATION: 28 cm. (fol.): π1 A² B–C⁸. [38] p.

NOTES: There are two known issues of this work, the second of which, contains numerous typographical errors on leaf B; cf. Alden. Illustrated title page. "La relacio[n] del viage que hizo el señor capitan Herna[n]do Piçarro . . ." signed: Miguel Estete (p. [26–33]).

REFERENCES: JCB Lib. cat., pre-1675, I, p. 116; Alden, *European Americana*, 534/35; Medina, *Bib. hispano-americana*, 95.

JCB LIBRARY COPY: Acquired in 1911. This copy is the issue with the typographical errors on leaf B; closely trimmed with slight loss of text.

COPIES: NN, CSmH, RPJCB.

## 27

ZÁRATE, AGUSTÍN DE, b. 1514.

Historia del descubrimiento y conquista del Peru, con las cosas naturales que señaladamente alli se hallan, y los sucessos que ha auido. La qual escriuia Augustin de Çarate, exerciendo el cargo de contador general de cuentas por Su Magestad en aquella prouincia, y en la de Tierra Firme.

En Anuers en casa de Martin Nucio, a los dos cigueñas. Año M.D.LV. [1555]

COLLATION: 15 cm. (8vo): *⁸ A–2M⁸. [8], 273, [7] leaves; ill.

NOTES: Title vignette: printer's device with motto: Pietas homini tutissima virtus.

REFERENCES: JCB Lib. cat., pre-1675, I, p. 189; Alden, *European Americana*, 555/50; Medina, *Bib. hispano-americana*, 173.

JCB LIBRARY COPY: Acquired before 1865. This copy lacks leaves [1–7] at end; available in facsimile.

COPIES: DLC, PPRF, NN, NjP, RPJCB, CSmH.

# EDITIONS AND TRANSLATIONS

Acosta, José de. *Historia natural y moral de las Indias*. Seville: J. de León, 1590.
——Barcelona: J. Cendrat, 1591.
——Madrid: A. Martín, for J. Berrillo, 1608.
——Madrid: P. Aznar, for A. del Castillo, 1792.
—*Historia naturale, e morale delle Indie*. Venice: B. Basa, 1596.
—*Historie naturael ende morael van de Westersche Indien*. Haarlem: G. Rooman, for J. L. Meyn, at Enkhuizen, 1598.
——Amsterdam: B. Janszoon, 1624.
—*Histoire naturelle et moralle des Indes*. Paris: M. Orry, 1598.
——Paris: M. Orry, 1600.
——Paris: M. Orry, 1606.
——Paris: A. Tiffaine, 1616.
——Paris: A. Tiffaine, 1617.
—[German translation]. [Frankfurt a. M.: W. Richter, 1601] *in:* Acosta, José de. *Neundter und letzter Theil Americae* (Theodor de Bry's America. Pt. 9. German). Frankfurt a. M.: W. Richter & M. Becker, 1601.
—*America, oder wie mans zu teutsch nennet die Neuwe Welt, oder West India*. Oberursel: C. Sutor, 1605.
—[Latin translation]. [Frankfurt a. M.: M. Becker, 1602] *in:* Acosta, José de. *Americae nona & postrema pars* (Theodor de Bry's America. Pt. 9. Latin). Frankfurt a. M.: M. Becker, 1602.
—*The naturall and moral historie of the East and West Indies*. London: V. Simmes, for E. Blount & W. Aspley, 1604.

Acuña, Cristóbal de. *Nuevo descubrimiento del gran rio de las Amazonas*. Madrid: Imprenta Real, 1641.
—*Relation de la riviere des Amazonas*. Paris: C. Barbin, 1682.
——[Amsterdam: Widow of P. Marret, 1716] *in:* Rogers, Woodes. *Voyage autour du monde*. Amsterdam: Widow of P. Marret, 1716.
—*Relazione del rio, ò fiume delle Amazoni*. [Parma: I. & F. M. Rosati, 1691] *in:* Zani, Valerio. *Il genio vagante biblioteca curiosa*. Parma: G. dall Oglio & I. Rosati, 1691–1693.
—*A relation of the great river of Amazons*. [London: S. Buckley, 1698] *in: Voyages and discoveries in South-America*. London: S. Buckley, 1698.
—*Bericht von dem Strom derer Amazonen*. [Vienna: P. Straub, 1729] *in:* Vandiera, Domenico. *Erbauliche und angenehme Geschichten derer Chiquitos*. Vienna: P. Straub, 1729.
——[Vienna: P. Straub, 1733] *in:* Vandiera, Domenico. *Neuer Welt-Bot*. Vienna: P. Straub, 1733.

Albenino, Nicolao de. *Verdadera relacion*. Seville: J. de León, 1549.

Anghiera, Pietro Martire d'. *De orbe novo*. [Decades 1–3] Alcalá de Henares: A. G. Brocar, for A. de Nebrija, 1516.
—*De nuper sub D. Carolo repertis insulis*. [Decade 4] Basel: [A. Petri], 1521.
—*De rebus, et insulis noviter repertis*. [Decade 4] [Nuremberg: F. Peypus, 1524] *in:* Cortés, Hernán. *De nova maris oceani Hyspania*. Nuremberg: F. Peypus, 1524.
—*De insulis nuper inventis*. [Decade 4] [Cologne: M. von Neuss, for A. Birckmann, 1532] *in:* Cortés, Hernán. *De insulis nuper inventis*. Cologne: M. von Neuss, for A. Birckmann, 1532.
——[Antwerp: J. Steels, 1536] *in:* Burchardus, de Monte Sion. *Descriptio terrae sanctae exactissima*. Antwerp: J. Steels, 1536.
—*Von Geschichten unnd Inseln newlich . . . erfunden*. [Decade 4] [Augsburg: P. Ulhart, 1550] *in:* Cortés, Hernán. *Von dem Newen Hispanien*. Augsburg: P. Ulhart, 1550.
—*Extraict ou recueil des isles nouvellement trouvees*. [Decades 1–4] Paris: S. de Colines, 1532.
—*De rebus oceanicis & orbe novo*. [Decades 1–4] Basel: J. Bebel, 1533.
——Cologne: G. Calenius & heirs of J. Quentel, 1574.
—*Libro primo della historia de l'Indie Occidentali*.

ANGHIERA (*cont.*)

[Decades 1–4] [Venice, 1534] *in: Summario de la generale historia de l'Indie Occidentali.* Venice, 1534.

— *The decades of the Newe Worlde.* [Decades 1–4] London: W. Powell & E. Sutton, 1555.

—— London: W. Powell & R. Toye, 1555.

— *Ander Theil, der Newen Welt.* [Decades 1–4] Basel: S. Henricpetri, 1582 *in:* BENZONI, Girolamo. *Erste Theil, der Newenn Weldt.* Basel: S. Henricpetri, 1582.

— *De orbe novo.* [Decades 1–8] Alcalá de Henares: M. de Eguía, 1530.

—— Paris: G. Auvray, 1587.

— *The history of travayle in the West and East Indies.* [Decades 1–8] London: R. Jugge, 1577.

— *De novo orbe, or The historie of the West Indies.* [Decades 1–8] London: T. Adams, 1612.

— *The historie of the West-Indies.* [Decades 1–8] London: A. Hebb, [1625?].

— *The famous historie of the Indies.* [Decades 1–8] London: M. Sparke, 1628.

BARCO CENTENERA, Martín del. *Argentina y conquista del Rio de la Plata.* Lisbon: P. Crasbeeck, 1602.

—— [Madrid, 1749] *in:* BARCIA CARBALLIDO Y ZÚÑIGA, Andrés González de. *Historiadores primitivos de las Indias Occidentales.* Madrid, 1749.

CALANCHA, Antonio de la. *Coronica moralizada del orden de San Augustin en el Peru.* Barcelona: P. Lacavallería, 1639.

CASAS, Bartolomé de las. *Brevissima relacion.* Seville: S. Trugillo, 1552–1553. (*This collection of nine tracts is known as Brevissima relacion, which is also the title of the first tract. Most of the editions and translations noted below, however, do not contain the complete collection, but rather consist of the first piece with portions of the other tracts sometimes appended.*)

— *Las obras.* [6 of 9 tracts] Barcelona: A. Lacavallería, 1646.

— *Seer cort verhael vande destructie van d'Indien.* [Antwerp?], 1578.

— *Spieghel der Spaenscher tyrannye in West Indien.* Amsterdam: N. Biestkens 'de Jonge', for C. Claeszoon, 1596.

—— Amsterdam: C. Claeszoon, 1607.

—— Amsterdam: Widow of C. Claeszoon, 1610.

—— Amsterdam: J. E. Cloppenburg, 1620 [i.e. *c.* 1622?].

—— Amsterdam: E. Cloppenburg, 1638.

—— Amsterdam: I. van der Putte, [between 1710 and 1748].

— *Den vermeerderden spieghel der Spaensche tierannije.* Amsterdam: C. L. van der Plasse, 1621.

—— Amsterdam: C. L. van der Plasse, 1623.

—— Amsterdam: C. L. van der Plasse, 1634.

—— Amsterdam: G. J. Saeghman, 1664.

— *Tyrannies et cruautez des espagnols.* Antwerp: F. Raphelengius, 1579.

—— Paris: G. Julien, 1582.

—— Rouen: J. Cailloué, 1630.

— *Histoire admirable des horribles insolences.* [Geneva]: G. Cartier, 1582.

— *Le miroir de la tyrannie espagnole.* Amsterdam: J. E. Cloppenburg, 1620.

—— Amsterdam: J. E. Cloppenburg, 1620 *in:* GYPSIUS, Johannes. *Le miroir de la cruelle & horrible tyrannie espagnole.* Amsterdam: J. E. Cloppenburg, 1620.

— *Histoire des Indes Occidentales.* Lyons: J. Caffin & F. Plaignard, 1642.

— *La decouverte des Indes Occidentales.* Paris: A. Pralard, 1697.

—— Paris: D. Mariette, 1701.

— *Relation des voyages et des découvertes.* Amsterdam: J. L. de Lorme, 1698.

— *The Spanish colonie.* London: T. Dawson, for W. Brome, 1583.

— *The tears of the Indians.* London: J. C., for N. Brooke, 1656.

— *Popery truly display'd.* London: R. Hewson, 1689.

— *An account of the first voyages and discoveries made by the Spaniards in America.* London: J. Darby, for D. Brown, J. Harris, and A. Bell, 1699.

— *Popery and slavery display'd.* London: C. Corbett, 1745.

— *Newe Welt.* [Frankfurt a. M.], 1597.

—— [Frankfurt a. M.], 1599.

— *Warhafftiger und gründtlicher Bericht.* [Frankfurt a. M., 1599].

—— Oppenheim: J. T. de Bry, 1613.

— *Umbständige warhaffte Beschreibung der indianischen Ländern.* [Heidelberg?: W. Walter?], 1665.

— *Die Verheerung Westindiens.* Berlin: C. F. Himburg, 1790.

— *Narratio regionum Indicarum per Hispanos.* Frankfurt a. M.: T. de Bry & J. Sauer, 1598.
— — Oppenheim: H. Galler, for J. T. de Bry, 1614.
— *Regionum Indicarum per Hispanos ... descriptio.* Heidelberg: W. Walter, 1664.
— *Istoria ò brevissima relatione.* Venice: M. Ginammi, 1626.
— — Venice: M. Ginammi, 1630.
— — Venice: M. Ginammi, 1643.

CASTELLANOS, Juan de. *Primera parte, de las elegias de varones illustres de Indias.* Madrid: Widow of A. Gómez, 1589.

CIEZA DE LEÓN, Pedro de. *Parte primera de la chronica del Peru.* Seville: M. de Montesdoca, 1553.
— — Antwerp: H. de Laet, for J. Bellère, 1554.
— — Antwerp: H. de Laet, for J. Steels, 1554.
— — Antwerp: M. Nuyts, 1554.
— *La prima parte de la cronica del ... Peru.* Rome: V. & L. Dorici, 1555.
— — Venice: F. Lorenzini, 1560.
— — Venice: C. Franceschini, 1576.
— *La prima parte dell' istorie del Peru.* Venice: D. Farri, for A. Arrivabene, 1556.
— — Venice: G. Ziletti, 1557.
— — Venice: G. Ziletti, 1560.
— *Historia, over cronica del gran regno del Peru.* Venice: G. Bonadio, 1564.
— *The seventeen years travels ... through ... Peru.* London, 1709 *in:* STEVENS, John. *A new collection of voyages and travels.* London: J. Knapton, J. Round, N. Cliff, E. Sanger, & A. Collins, 1708–1710; and *in:* STEVENS, John. *A new collection of voyages and travels.* London: J. Knapton, A. Bell, D. Midwinter, W. Taylor, A. Collins, & J. Baker, 1711.

COLÓN, Fernando. *Historie ... della vita, & de' fatti dell' ammiraglio D. Christoforo Colombo.* Venice: F. de' Franceschi, 1571.
— — Milan: G. Bordone, [1614].
— — Venice: G. P. Brigonci, 1676.
— — Venice: Prodocimo, 1678.
— — Venice: G. Tramontin, 1685.
— — Venice: Prodocimo, 1709.
— — Venice: Lovisa, 1728.
— *La vie de Cristofle Colomb.* Paris: C. Barbin & C. Ballard, 1681.
— *The history of the life and actions of Adm. Christopher Columbus.* [London: A. & J. Churchill, 1704] *in:* CHURCHILL, Awnsham. *A collection of voyages and travels.* London: A. & J. Churchill, 1704.
— *La historia ... de la vida, y hechos de el almirante D. Christoval Colón.* [Madrid, 1749] *in:* BARCIA CARBALLIDO Y ZÚÑIGA, Andrés González de. *Historiadores primitivos de las Indias Occidentales.* Madrid, 1749.

COLUMBUS, Christopher. *Epistola.* [Rome: S. Plannck, 1493] [34 lines to page].
— — [Rome: S. Plannck, 1493] [33 lines to page].
— — Rome: E. Silber, 1493.
— — [Basel: J. Wolff, 1493].
— — Paris: [G. Marchant, 1493].
— — [Basel: J. Bergmann, 1494] *in:* VERARDI, Carlo. *In laudem ... Ferdinandi Hispaniarum regis.* Basel: J. Bergmann, 1494.
— — [Basel: H. Petri, 1533] *in:* ROBERTUS, Monarchus. *Bellum Christianorum principum.* Basel: H. Petri, 1533.
— — [Frankfurt a. M.: C. de Marne & Heirs of J. Aubry, 1603–1608] *in:* SCHOTTUS, Andreas. *Hispaniae illustratae, seu rerum urbiumque Hispaniae, Lusitaniae, Aethiopiae, et Indiae scriptores varii.* Frankfurt a. M.: C. de Marne & Heirs of J. Aubry, 1603–1608.
— *Eyn schön hübsch Lesen von etlichen Insslen.* Strassburg: B. Kistler, 1497.

CÓRDOVA SALINAS, Diego de. *Vida, virtudes, y milagros del apostol ... Francisco Solano.* Madrid: Imprenta Real, 1676.
— *Leben/ Tugenden/ unnd Wunderwerck/ dess Apostels von Peru.* Munich: J. Jäcklin, 1676.

CORTÉS, Hernán. *Carta de relacion.* [2nd letter] Seville: J. Cromberger, 1522.
— — Saragossa: J. Coci, 1523.
— — [Madrid, 1749] *in:* BARCIA CARBALLIDO Y ZÚÑIGA, Andrés González de. *Historiadores primitivos de las Indias Occidentales.* Madrid, 1749.
— — [Mexico: J. A. de Hogal, 1770] *in:* CORTÉS, Hernán. *Historia de Nueva España.* Mexico: J. A. de Hogal, 1770.
— *Praeclara ... de nova maris oceani.* Nuremberg: F. Peypus, 1524.
— — [Cologne: Melchior von Neuss, for A. Birckmann, 1532] *in:* CORTÉS, Hernán. *De insulis nuper*

CORTÉS (cont.)
    *inventis*. Cologne: Melchior von Neuss, for A. Birckmann, 1532.
—— [Basel: J. Herwagen, 1555] *in: Novus orbus regionum*. Basel: J. Herwagen, 1555.
— *La preclara narratione . . . della Nuova Hispagna*. Venice: B. Vercellensis, for G. B. Pederzano, 1524.
— [French translation]. [Paris: S. de Colines, 1532] *in:* ANGHIERA, Pietro Martire d'. *Extraict ou recueil des isles nouvellement trouveés*. Paris: S. de Colines, 1532.
—— [Paris: Cellot & Jombert, 1778] *in:* CORTÉS, Hernán. *Correspondance*. Paris: Cellot & Jombert, 1778.
—— [Switzerland: Libraires Associés, 1779] *in:* CORTÉS, Hernán. *Correspondance*. Switzerland: Libraires Associés, 1779.
— [German translation]. [Augsburg: P. Ulhart, 1550] *in:* CORTÉS, Hernán. *Von dem Newen Hispanien*. Augsburg: P. Ulhart, 1550.
—— [Heidelberg: Pfähler Brothers, 1779] *in:* CORTÉS, Hernán. *Briefe*. Heidelberg: Pfähler Brothers, 1779.
— [Dutch translation]. [Amsterdam: Yntema & Tieboel, 1780] *in:* CORTÉS, Hernán. *Brieven*. Amsterdam: Yntema & Tieboel, 1780.

CORTÉS, Hernán. *Carta tercera*. Seville: J. Cromberger, 1523.
—— [Madrid, 1749] *in:* BARCIA CARBALLIDO Y ZÚÑIGA, Andrés González de. *Historiadores primitivos de las Indias Occidentales*. Madrid, 1749.
—— [Mexico: J. A. de Hogal, 1770] *in:* CORTÉS, Hernán. *Historia de Nueva España*. Mexico: J. A. de Hogal, 1770.
— *Tercia . . . in nova maris Oceani Hyspania generalis praefecti praeclara narratio*. Nuremberg: F. Peypus, 1524.
—— [Cologne: Melchior von Neuss, for A. Birckmann, 1532] *in:* CORTÉS, Hernán. *De insulis nuper inventis*. Cologne: Melchior von Neuss, for A. Birckmann, 1532.
—— [Basel: J. Herwagen, 1555] *in: Novus Orbus regionum*. Basel: J. Herwagen, 1555.
— [French translation]. [Paris: S. de Colines, 1532] *in:* ANGHIERA, Pietro Martire d'. *Extraict ou recueil des isles nouvellement trouvées*. Paris: S. de Colines, 1532.
—— [Paris: Cellot & Jombert, 1778] *in:* CORTÉS, Hernán. *Correspondance*. Paris: Cellot & Jombert, 1778.
—— [Switzerland: Libraires Associés, 1779] *in:* CORTÉS, Hernán. *Correspondance*. Switzerland: Libraires Associés, 1779.
— [German translation]. [Augsburg: P. Ulhart, 1550] *in:* CORTÉS, Hernán. *Von dem Newen Hispanien*. Augsburg: P. Ulhart, 1550.
—— [Heidelberg: Pfähler Brothers, 1779] *in:* CORTÉS, Hernán. *Briefe*. Heidelberg: Pfähler Brothers, 1779.
— [Dutch translation]. [Amsterdam: Yntema & Tieboel, 1780] *in:* CORTÉS, Hernán. *Brieven*. Amsterdam: Yntema & Tieboel, 1780.

CORTÉS, Hernán. *La quarta relacion*. Toledo: G. de Avila, 1525.
—— Valencia: G. Costilla, 1526.
—— [Madrid, 1749] *in:* BARCIA CARBALLIDO Y ZÚÑIGA, Andrés González de. *Historiadores primitivos de las Indias Occidentales*. Madrid, 1749.
—— [Mexico: J. A. de Hogal, 1770] *in:* CORTÉS, Hernán. *Historia de Nueva España*. Mexico: J. A. de Hogal, 1770.
— [Dutch translation]. [Amsterdam: Yntema & Tieboel, 1780] *in:* CORTÉS, Hernán. *Brieven*. Amsterdam: Yntema & Tieboel, 1780.
— [French translation]. [Paris: Cellot & Jombert, 1778] *in:* CORTÉS, Hernán. *Correspondance*. Paris: Cellot & Jombert, 1778.
—— [Switzerland: Libraires Associés, 1779] *in:* CORTÉS, Hernán. *Correspondance*. Switzerland: Libraires Associés, 1779.
— [German translation]. [Heidelberg: Pfähler Brothers, 1779] *in:* CORTÉS, Hernán. *Briefe*. Heidelberg: Pfähler Brothers, 1779.

CUBERO SEBASTIÁN, Pedro. *Peregrinacion del mundo*. Naples: C. Porsile, 1682.

DÁVILA PADILLA, Agustín. *Historia de la fundacion . . . de la provincia de Santiago de Mexico*. Madrid: P. Madrigal, 1596.
—— Brussels: J. van Meerbeeck, 1625.
— *Varia historia de la Nueva España y Florida*. Valladolid: J. B. Varesio, 1634.

DÍAZ DEL CASTILLO, Bernal. *Historia verdadera de la conquista de la Nueva España*. Madrid: Imprenta Real, [1632]

—— Madrid: B. Cano, 1795–1796.
— *The true history of the conquest of Mexico.* London: J. Wright, 1800.

ENCISO, Martín Fernández de. *Suma de geographia.* Seville: J. Cromberger, 1519.
—— Seville: J. Cromberger, 1530.
—— Seville: A. de Burgos, 1546.

ERCILLA Y ZÚÑIGA, Alonso de. *La Araucana.* [Pt. 1] Salamanca: D. de Portonariis, for V. & S. de Portonariis, 1574.
—— Lisbon: A. Ribeiro, 1582.
—— Madrid: Widow of A. Gómez, 1585.
—— [Pt. 2] Saragossa: J. Soler, 1578.
—— [Lisbon]: A. Ribeiro, 1588.
—— [Pts. 1–2] Madrid: P. Cosín, 1578.
—— [Pts. 1–3] Madrid: P. Madrigal, 1590.
—— Barcelona: Widow of H. Gotart, for S. de Cormellas & G. Lloberas, 1592.
—— Antwerp: A. Bacx, for P. Bellère, 1597.
—— Madrid: Imprenta Real, 1632.
—— Madrid: F. Martínez Abad, 1733.
—— Madrid: A. de Sancha, 1776.
— *Historiale beschrijvinghe der goudtrijcke landen in Chili ende Arauco.* [Pts. 1–3] Rotterdam: J. van Waesberghe, 1619.

FERNÁNDEZ, Diego. *Primera, y segunda parte, de la historia del Peru.* Seville: F. Díaz, 1571.

FERNÁNDEZ DE MEDRANO, Sebastián. *Breve descripcion del mundo.* Brussels: Heirs of F. Foppens, 1686.
—— Brussels: L. Marchant, 1688.
—— Brussels: L. Marchant; Barcelona: J. Texidor, 1688.
—— Cadiz: C. de Requeña, 1693.

FERNÁNDEZ DE OVIEDO Y VALDÉS, Gonzalo. *De la natural hystoria de las Indias.* Toledo: R. de Petras, 1526.
— *Relacion sumaria de la historia natural de las Indias.* [Madrid, 1749] *in:* BARCIA CARBALLIDO Y ZÚÑIGA, Andrés González de. *Historiadores primitivos de las Indias Occidentales.* Madrid, 1749.
— *Libro secondo delle Indie Occidentali.* [Venice, 1534] *in: Summario de la generale historia de l'Indie Occidentali.* Venice, 1534.
— [Turkish translation]. [Constantinople: I. Mutafarrika, at the Imperial Press, 1730] *in:* [*Ta'rikh al-Hind al-Gharbi*]. Constantinople: I. Mutafarrika, at the Imperial Press, 1730.

FERNÁNDEZ DE OVIEDO Y VALDÉS, Gonzalo. *La historia general de las Indias.* Seville: J. Cromberger, 1535.
—— [Salamanca: J. de Junta, 1547] *in:* FERNÁNDEZ DE OVIEDO Y VALDÉS, Gonzalo. *Coronica de las Indias.* Salamanca: J. de Junta, 1547.
— *L'histoire naturelle et generalle des Indes.* Paris: M. de Vascovan, 1555.
—— Paris: M. de Vascovan, 1556.
— *History of the West Indies.* [London: R. Jug, 1557] *in:* ANGHIERA, Pietro Martire d'. *The history of travayle in the West and East Indies.* London: R. Jug, 1577.

FERNÁNDEZ DE PIEDRAHITA, Lucas. *Historia general de las conquistas.* Antwerp: J. B. Verdussen [i.e. Seville: T. López de Haro?], [1688].

FLORES, Bartolomé de. *Obra nuevamente compuesta.* Seville: F. Díaz, 1571.

GARCÍA, Gregorio. *Origen de los Indios de el Nuevo Mundo.* Valencia: P. P. Mey, 1607.
—— Madrid: F. Martínez Abad, 1729.

GRIJALVA, Juan de. *Cronica de la orden de N. P. S. Augustin en las provincias de la Nueva España.* Mexico: J. Ruiz, 1624.

HERRERA Y TORDESILLAS, Antonio de. *Historia general de los hechos de los castellanos.* Madrid: J. Flamenco & J. de la Cuesta, for the Imprenta Real, 1601–1615. (*In addition to the eight decades, this work also contains Descripcion des Indes Occidentales. Separately issued editions and translations of the latter are not included below.*)
—— Madrid: F. Martínez Abad, for N. Rodríguez Franco, 1730.
— *Historia general de las Indes Occidentales.* Antwerp: J. B. Verdussen, 1728.
— *Histoire generale des voyages . . . des Castillans.* [Decades 1–3] Paris: N. & J. de la Coste, 1660–1671.
— [Dutch translation]. [Selections] [Leyden: P. van der Aa, 1706–1707] *in:* AA, Pieter van der. *Naaukeurige versameling der gedenk-waardigste.* Leyden: P. van der Aa, 1707–1708.
— *The general history of the vast continent and islands*

HERRARA Y TORDESILLAS (*cont.*)
*of America*. [Decades 1–8] London: J. Batley, 1725–1726.

JARQUE, Francisco. *Insignes missioneros de la Compañia de Jesus en... Paraguay*. Pamplona: J. Micón, 1687.

LASSO DE LA VEGA, Gabriel. *Primera parte de Cortés valeroso, y Mexicana*. Madrid: P. Madrigal, 1588.
— *Mexicana*. Madrid: L. Sanchéz, 1594.

*Libro ultimo del summario delle Indie Occidentali*. Venice, 1534 *in: Summario de la generale historia de l'Indie Occidentali*. Venice, 1534.
— *Relatione di un capitano spagnuolo della conquista del Peru*. [Venice: Heirs of L. Giunta, 1556] *in:* RAMUSIO, Giovanni Battista. *Terzo volume delle navigationi et viaggi*. Venice: Heirs of L. Giunta, 1556.
— — [Venice: Heirs of L. Giunta, 1565] *in:* RAMUSIO, Giovanni Battista. *Terzo volume delle navigationi et viaggi*. Venice: Heirs of L. Giunta, 1565.
— — [Venice: The Giuntas, 1606] *in:* RAMUSIO, Giovanni Battista. *Terzo volume delle navigationi et viaggi*. Venice: The Giuntas, 1606.
— *L'histoire de la terre neuve du Perù en l'Inde Occidentale*. Paris: P. Gaultier, for J. Barbé & V. Sertenas, 1545.

LOPEZ DE COGOLLUDO, Diego. *Historia de Yucathan*. Madrid: J. García Infanzón, 1688.

LÓPEZ DE GÓMARA, Francisco. *La istoria de las Indias* [Pt. 1] *y Conquista de Mexico* [Pt. 2]. Saragossa: A. Millán, 1552.
— *Hispania victrix*. [Pts. 1–2] Medina del Campo: G. de Millis, 1553.
— *Primera y segunda parte de la historia general de las Indias*. Saragossa: A. Millán, for M. Capila, 1553.
— *La historia general de las Indias*. [Pts. 1–2] Antwerp: H. de Laet, for J. Steels, 1554.
— — Antwerp: H. de Laet, for J. Bellère, 1554.
— — Antwerp: M. Nuyts, 1554.
— — Saragossa: P. Bernuz & A. Millán, for M. de Zapila, 1554.
— — Saragossa: P. Bernuz & A. Millán, for M. de Zapila, 1555.
— — [Madrid, 1749] *in:* BARCIA CARBALLIDO Y ZÚÑIGA, Andrés González de. *Historiadores primitivos de las Indias Occidentales*. Madrid, 1749.
— *La historia generale delle Indie Occidentali*. [Pts. 1–2] Rome: V. & L. Dorici, 1556.
— *Historia di Mexico*. [Pt. 2] Rome: V. & L. Dorici, 1555 [i.e. 1556].
— *La seconda parte delle historie dell' India*. [Pt. 1] Venice: D. Farri, for A. Arrivabene, 1557 *issued as a continuation of:* CIEZA DE LEÓN, Pedro. *La prima parte dell' istorie del Peru*. Venice: D. Farri, for A. Arrivabene, 1556.
— — D. Farri, for G. Ziletti, 1557 *issued as a continuation of:* CIEZA DE LEÓN, Pedro. *La prima parte dell' istorie del Peru*. Venice: G. Ziletti, 1557.
— — [Pts. 1–2] Venice: G. Ziletti, 1565–1566 *issued as a continuation of:* CIEZA DE LEÓN, Pedro. *La prima parte dell' historie del Peru*. Venice: G. Ziletti, 1560.
— *Historia delle nuove Indie Occidentali*. [Pts. 1–2] Venice: F. Lorenzini, 1560 *issued as a continuation of:* CIEZA DE LEÓN, Pedro. *Cronica del gran regno del Peru*. Venice: F. Lorenzini, 1560.
— — [Pt. 1] Venice: G. Bonadio, 1564 *issued as a continuation of:* CIEZA DE LEÓN, Pedro. *Historia, over cronica del gran regno del Peru*. Venice: G. Bonadio, 1564.
— — [Pts. 1–2] Venice: C. Franceschini, 1576 *issued as a continuation of:* CIEZA DE LEÓN, Pedro. *Cronica del gran regno del Peru*. Venice: C. Franceschini, 1576.
— *Historia dell' Indie Occidentali*. [Pt. 2] Venice: B. Barezzi, 1599.
— *Histoire generalle des Indes Occidentales*. [Pt. 1] Paris: M. Sonnius, 1569.
— — Paris: B. Turrisan, 1569.
— — Paris: M. Sonnius, 1577.
— — Paris: M. Sonnius, 1578.
— — Paris: M. Sonnius, 1580.
— — [Pts. 1–2] Paris: M. Sonnius, 1584.
— — [Pts. 1–2] Paris: M. Sonnius, 1587.
— — [Pts. 1–2] Paris: M. Sonnius, 1605.
— — [Pts. 1–2] Paris: M. Sonnius, 1606.
— *Voyages et conquestes du Capitaine Ferdinand Courtois*. [Pt. 2] Paris: A. L'Angelier, 1588.
— *The pleasant historie of the conquest of the Weast India*. [Pt. 2] Paris: H. Bynneman, [1578].
— — London: T. Creede, 1596.
— [*Ta'rikh al-Hind al-Gharbi*]. [Pts. 1–2] Constantinople: I. Mutafarrika & Imperial Press, 1730.

MELÉNDEZ, Juan. *Tesoros verdaderos de las Yndias.* Rome: N. Tinassi, 1681–1682.

MONARDES, Nicolás. *Dos libros.* [Pt. 1] Seville: S. Trugillo, 1565.
—— Seville: F. Díaz, 1569.
— *Della historia de i semplici, aromati, et altre cose.* [Pt. 1] [Venice, 1576] *in:* ORTA, Garcia de. *Due libri dell' historia de i semplici.* Venice, 1576.
— *Segunda parte del libro, de las cosas que se traen de nuestras Indias Occidentales.* [Pt. 2] Seville: A. Escrivano, 1571.
— *De simplicibus medicamentis ex Occidentali India delatis.* [Pts. 1–2] Antwerp: C. Plantin, 1574.
— *Delle cose, che vengono portate dall' Indie Occidentali.* [Pts. 1–2] Venice: G. Ziletti, 1575.
—— Venice: G. Ziletti, 1582.
—— [Venice: Heirs of F. Ziletti, 1589] *in:* ORTA, Garcia de. *Dell' historia de i semplici aromati.* Venice: Heirs of F. Ziletti, 1589.
—— [Venice: G. Salis, 1616] *in:* ORTA, Garcia de. *Dell' historia de i semplici aromati.* Venice: G. Salis, 1616.
— *Primera y segunda y tercera partes de la historia medicinal.* [Pts. 1–3] Seville: A. Escrivano, 1574.
—— Seville: F. Díaz, 1580.
— *Joyfull newes out of the newe founde worlde.* [Pts. 1–3] London: W. Norton, 1577.
—— London: W. Norton, 1580.
—— London: E. Allde, assigns of B. Norton, 1596.
— *Simplicium medicamentorum ex Novo Orbe delatorum.* [Pts. 1–3] Antwerp: Widow of C. Plantin & J. Mourentorff, 1593 *in:* ORTA, Garcia de. *Aromatum, et simplicium.* Antwerp: Widow of C. Plantin & J. Mourentorff, 1593.
— *Histoire des simples medicamens.* [Pts. 1–3] Lyons: J. Pillehotte, 1602 *in:* ORTA, Garcia de. *Histoire des drogues espiceries.* Lyons: J. Pillehotte, 1602.
—— Lyons: J. Pillehotte, 1619 *in:* ORTA, Garcia de. *Histoire des drogues espiceries.* Lyons: J. Pillehotte, 1619.

MORGA, Antonio de. *Sucesos de las islas Filipinas.* Mexico: J. Balli, for C. A. César, 1609.

NÚÑEZ CABEZA DE VACA, Alvar. *La relacion.* [Pt. 1] Zamora: A. de Paz & J. Picardo, for J. P. Musetti, 1542.
— *La relacion y comentarios.* [Pts. 1–2] Valladolid: F. Fernández de Córdova, 1555.

— *Naufragios.* [Pt. 1] [Madrid, 1749] *in:* BARCIA CARBALLIDO Y ZÚÑIGA, Andrés González de. *Historiadores primitivos de las Indias Occidentales.* Madrid, 1749.
— *Comentarios.* [Pt. 2] [Madrid, 1749] *in:* BARCIA CARBALLIDO Y ZÚÑIGA, Andrés González de. *Historiadores primitivos de las Indias Occidentales.* Madrid, 1749.

OÑA, Pedro de. *Primera parte de Arauco domado.* Lima: A. Ricardo, 1596.
—— Madrid: J. de la Cuesta, for F. López, 1605.

ORDÓÑEZ DE CEVALLOS, Pedro. *Viage del mundo.* Madrid: L. Sanchez, 1614.
— *Historia, y viage del mundo.* Madrid: J. Garcia Infanzon, for J. Vascones, 1691.

OVALLE, Alonso de. *Historica relacion del reyno de Chile.* Rome: F. Cavalli, 1646.
— *Historica relatione del regno di Cile.* Rome: F. Cavalli, 1646.
— *Historical relation of the kingdom of Chile.* London: A. & J. Churchill, 1703.

PARRA, Jacinto de. *Rosa laureada entre los santos.* Madrid: D. García Morrás, 1670.

PIZARRO Y ORELLANA, Fernando. *Varones ilustres del Nuevo Mundo.* Madrid: D. Díaz de la Carrera, for P. Coello, 1639.

*Relatione di alcune cose della Nuova Spagna, & della gran città di Temestitan Messico.* [Venice: Heirs of L. Giunta, 1556] *in:* RAMUSIO, Giovanni Battista. *Terzo volume delle navigationi et viaggi.* Venice: Heirs of L. Giunta, 1556.
—— [Venice: Heirs of L. Giunta, 1565 *in:* RAMUSIO, Giovanni Battista. *Terzo volume delle navigationi et viaggi.* Venice: Heirs of L. Giunta, 1565.
—— [Venice: The Giuntas, 1606 *in:* RAMUSIO, Giovanni Battista. *Terzo volume delle navigationi et viaggi.* Venice: The Giuntas, 1606.

REMESAL, Antonio de. *Historia general de las Indias Ocidentales.* Madrid: F. Abarca de Angulo, 1620.

RODRÍGUEZ, Manuel. *El Marañon, y Amazonas.* Madrid: A. González de Reyes, 1684.

RUIZ DE MONTOYA, Antonio. *Conquista espiritual.* Madrid: Imprenta Real, 1639.

SÁNCHEZ DE AGUILAR, Pedro. *Informe contra idolorum cultores del obispado de Yucatan.* Madrid: Widow of J. González, 1639.

SANCHO, Pedro. *Relatione per Sua Maesta di quel che nel conquisto & pacificatione di queste provincie della Nuova Castiglia.* [Venice: Heirs of L. Giunta, 1556] *in:* RAMUSIO, Giovanni Battista. *Terzo volume delle navigationi et viaggi.* Venice: Heirs of L. Giunta, 1556.
— — [Venice: Heirs of L. Giunta, 1565] *in:* RAMUSIO, Giovanni Battista. *Terzo volume delle navigationi et viaggi.* Venice: Heirs of L. Giunta, 1565.
— — [Venice: The Giuntas, 1606] *in:* RAMUSIO, Giovanni Battista. *Terzo volume delle navigationi et viaggi.* Venice: The Giuntas, 1606.

SARMIENTO DE GAMBOA, Pedro. *Viage al Estrecho de Magallanes.* Madrid: Imprenta Real, 1768.

SOLÍS, Antonio de. *Historia de la conquista de Mexico.* Madrid: B. de Villa-Diego, 1684.
— —Barcelona: J. Llopis, 1691.
— —Madrid: A. González de Reyes, for D. L. Ximenez & F. Laso, 1704.
— —Antwerp: J. B. Verdussen, [1705].
— —Brussels: F. Foppens, [1705].
— —Barcelona: J. Llopis, for J. Piferrer, J. Batlle, & J. Suria, 1711.
— —Brussels: M.-M. Bousquet & Co., 1741.
— —Madrid: J. de Zúñiga, for Fraternity of St. Jerome, 1748.
— —Barcelona: PP. Carmelitas Descalzos, 1766.
— —Barcelona: T. Piferrer, 1771.
— —Madrid: B. Román, 1776.
— —Madrid: A. de Sáncha, 1783–1784.
— —Madrid: A. Fernández, 1790.
— —Madrid: P. Barco López, 1791.
— —Madrid: B. Cano, 1798–1799.
— *Histoire de la conquête du Mexique.* Paris: J. Bouillerot, 1691.
— —Paris: R. Pépié, 1691.
— —The Hague: A. Moetjens, 1692.
— —Paris: La Compagnie, 1704.
— —Paris: J. & M. Guignard, 1704.
— —Paris: La Compagnie, 1714.
— —Paris: La Compagnie, 1730.
— —Paris: La Compagnie, 1759.
— *Istoria della conquista del Messico.* Florence: G. F. Cecchi, 1699.
— —Venice: A. Poletti, 1704.
— —Venice: A. Poletti, 1715.
— —Venice: A. Poletti, 1733.
— *The history of the conquest of Mexico.* London: T. Woodward, J. Hooker, & J. Peele, 1724.
— —London: T. Woodward & H. Lintot, 1738.
— *Historie om conquêten af Mexico.* Copenhagen: A. H. Godiche, 1747.
— *Geschichte von der Eroberung Mexico.* Copenhagen & Leipzig: G. C. Rothe, 1750–1751.

SOLÓRZANO PEREIRA, Juan de. *Disputationem de Indiarum iure.* Madrid: F. Martínez, 1629–1639.
— *De Indiarum iure.* Lyons: L. Anisson, 1672.
— —Madrid: Imprenta de la Gaceta, 1777.
— *Politica indiana.* Madrid: D. Díaz de la Carrera, 1648.
— —Antwerp: H. & C. Verdussen, 1703.
— —Madrid: M. Sacristán & G. Ramirez, 1736–1739.
— —Madrid: Imprenta de la Gaceta, 1776.

SUÁREZ DE FIGUEROA, Cristóbal. *Hechos de don Garcia Hurtado de Mendoza.* Madrid: Imprenta Real, 1613.
— —Madrid: Imprenta Real, 1616.

TAMARA, FRANCISCO. *El libro de las costumbres.* Antwerp: M. Nuyts, 1556.

TORQUEMADA, Juan de. *Ia [-IIIa] parte de los veynte y un libros rituales y monarchia yndiana.* Seville: M. Clavijo, 1615.
— —Madrid: N. Rodríguez Franco, 1723 [i.e. 1725].

TOVAR, Juan de. *Historia de la benida de los yndios.* [MS] [Between 1582 and 1587].

VALDÉS, Rodrigo de. *Poema heroyco hispano-latino panegyrico.* Madrid: A. Roman, 1687.

VARGAS MACHUCA, Bernardo de. *Milicia y descripcion de las Indias.* Madrid: P. Madrigal, 1599.

VEGA, Garcilaso de la. *La Florida del Ynca.* Lisbon: P. Craesbeeck, 1605.
— —Madrid: N. Rodríguez Franco, 1723.
— *Histoire de la Floride.* Paris: G. Clouzier, 1670.
— *Histoire de la conquête de la Floride.* Paris: G. Nyon, 1709 [v. 2, 1707].
— —Lille; Paris: G. Nyon, 1711 [v. 2, 1707].
— —Leyden: P. van der Aa, 1731.
— —[Amsterdam: J. F. Bernard, 1737] *in:* VEGA, Garcilaso de la. *Histoire des Yncas.* Amsterdam: J. F. Bernard, 1737.
— *Geschichte der Eroberung von Florida.* Zelle; Frankfurt; Leipzig, G. C. Gsellius, 1753.

VEGA (*cont.*)

— *Ferdinand von Soto. Oder erster Kriegszug der Spanier durch Florida.* Nordhausen: C. G. Gross, 1785.

— *Authentische Geschichte der Eroberung von Florida.* Leipzig: C. W. Schubarth, 1794.

VEGA, Garcilaso de la. *Primera parte de los commentarios reales.* Lisbon: P. Craesbeeck, 1609.

——Madrid: N. Rodríguez Franco, 1723.

— *Le commentaire royal.* [Pt. 1] Paris: A. Courbé, 1633.

— *Histoire des Yncas.* [Pt. 1] Amsterdam: J. Desbordes, 1715.

——Amsterdam: J. F. Bernard, 1737.

——Paris: Prault, junior, 1744.

— *Geschichte der Ynkas.* [Pt. 1] Nordhausen: K. G. Gross, 1798.

— *Historia general del Peru.* [Pt. 2] Córdoba: Widow of A. de Barrera, 1617.

——Madrid: N. Rodríguez Franco, 1722.

— *Histoire des guerres civiles.* [Pt. 2] Paris: A. Courbé & E. Couterot, 1650.

——Paris: S. Piget, 1658.

——Amsterdam: G. Kuyper, 1706.

— *The royal commentaries of Peru.* [Pts. 1–2] London: M. Flesher, for J. Tonson, 1688.

VESPUCCI, Amerigo. *Petri Francisci de Medicis salutem plurimam dicit.* [Paris: F. Baligaut & J. Lambert, 1503].

— *Mundus novus.* [Venice: G. B. Sessa, 1504].

——Augsburg: J. Otmar, 1504.

——[Rome: E. Silber, 1504].

——[Antwerp: W. Vorsterman, 1505].

——[Paris: U. Gering & B. Rembolt, 1506].

— *De ora antarctica.* Strassburg: M. Hupfuff, 1505.

— *Von der neü gefunden Region.* [Basel: M. Furter, 1505].

——[Nuremberg: W. Huber, 1506].

——Nuremberg: W. Huber, [1506].

— *Van der nieuwer werelt.* Antwerp: J. van Doesborch, [1507?].

VILLAGRÁ, Gaspar Pérez de. *Historia de la Nueva Mexico.* Alcalá de Henares: L. Martínez Grande, for B. López, 1610.

XEREZ, Francisco de. *Verdadera relacion de la conquista del Peru.* Seville: B. Pérez, 1534.

——Salamanca: J. de Junta, 1547 *in:* FERNÁNDEZ DE OVIEDO Y VALDÉS, Gonzalo. *Coronica de las Indias.* Salamanca: J. de Junta, 1547.

——[Madrid, 1749] *in:* BARCIA CARBALLIDO Y ZÚÑIGA, Andrés González de. *Historiadores primitivos de las Indias Occidentales.* Madrid, 1749.

— *Libro primo de la conquista del Peru.* Venice: S. dei Nicolini da Sabbio, 1535.

ZÁRATE, Agustín de. *Historia del descubrimiento y conquista del Peru.* Antwerp: M. Nuyts, 1555.

——Seville: A. Escrivano, [1578].

——[Madrid, 1749] *in:* BARCIA CARBALLIDO Y ZÚÑIGA, Andrés González de. Historiadores primitivos de las Indias Occidentales. Madrid, 1749.

— *De wonderlijcke ende warachtighe historie vant coninckrijck van Peru.* Antwerp: W. Silvius, for J. Verwithagen, 1563.

— *Conqueste van Indien.* Amsterdam: C. Claeszoon, 1596.

——Amsterdam: C. Claeszoon, 1598.

— *Le historie . . . dello scoprimento et conquista del Peru.* Venice: G. Giolito de' Ferrari, 1563.

— *The discoverie and conquest of the provinces of Peru.* London: R. Jones, 1581.

— *Histoire de la decouverte et de la conquete du Perou.* Amsterdam: J. L. de Lorme, 1700.

——Paris: C. Osmont, 1706.

——Paris: La Compagnie, 1716.

——Paris: M. Guignard, 1716.

——Amsterdam: J. L. de Lorme, 1717.

——Amsterdam: Duvillard & Changuion, 1719.

——Paris: La Compagnie, 1742.

——Paris: La Compagnie, 1774.

PRINTED BY THE STINEHOUR PRESS,
LUNENBURG, VERMONT
DESIGNED BY
MARK ARGETSINGER
ROCHESTER, NEW YORK

★